Holy Terrors
and
Gentle Souls

What lies behind us and what lies before us are tiny matters, compared to what lies within us.

Ralph Waldo Emerson

Holy Terrors

and

Gentle Souls

STORIES
ABOUT
THE
SAINTS

STEPHANIE WELLER HANSON

Saint Mary's Press
Christian Brothers Publications
Winona, Minnesota

Short Fiction Books from Saint Mary's Press

Waking Up Bees
STORIES OF LIVING LIFE'S QUESTIONS

Mountains of the Moon
STORIES ABOUT SOCIAL JUSTICE

The Centurion and the Songbird
STORIES ABOUT THE GOSPELS

  Genuine recycled paper with 10% post-consumer waste. Printed with soy-based ink.

The publishing team included Jerry Windley-Daoust, development editor; Mary Duerson, copy editor; Lynn Riska, production editor; Hollace Storkel, typesetter; Laurie Geisler, art director; Proof Positive/Farrowlyne Associates, Inc., series front cover designer; Abe Day, cover illustrator; manufactured by the production services department of Saint Mary's Press.

Printed in the United States of America

Printing: 9 8 7 6 5 4 3 2 1

Year: 2009 08 07 06 05 04 03 02 01

ISBN 0-88489-630-7

Library of Congress Cataloging-in-Publication Data

Hanson, Stephanie Weller.
    Holy terrors and gentle souls : stories about the saints / Stephanie Weller Hanson.
        p. cm.
    ISBN 0-88489-630-7 (pbk.)
    1. Christian saints—Fiction. 2. Christian fiction, American. I. Title.
PS3558.A543785 H36 2001
813'.54—dc21

                                                        2001001544

Contents

For the Sake
of What Will Come

Peter

Simon Peter was a Hebrew fisherman living in Galilee when Jesus called him. He worked with his brother Andrew, and with John, James, and their father, Zebedee. We know that Peter was married because of the story in Matthew about Jesus healing Peter's mother-in-law. It is reasonable to assume that Peter was relatively poor, and that he probably could not read or write. Yet Peter's personality shines through the New Testament. He was warmhearted and impetuous, a man always ready with an answer, even if it was the wrong one. Peter was a natural leader, and capable of radical insight, as in this story, but he could also be downright stubborn.

✦ ✦ ✦

The Master asked, "Who do the people say the Son of Man is?"

Silence. John and James stared at each other. Nathanael pulled the hood of his cloak low over his face as if to hide. Well, thought Peter, the March wind was cold. Jesus, in silence, looked north to the high road to Caesarea Philippi, and the three snow-covered peaks of Mount Hermon.

Andrew nudged Peter; but Peter didn't want to speak. The idea was there again, the one that had been humming in his mind for months as he watched the Master preach and heal. It was strange that as Jesus confronted the Pharisees, it only grew stronger.

Thaddaeus, stuttering a little, said, "Some s-say John the Baptist, others Elijah."

"Others say Jeremiah, or one of the prophets." That was Judas, watching from the edges as always.

Peter felt his face going red, as if he were trying to lift the tremendous weight of the idea. He wanted to speak, but he was afraid. Last week Judas had told him that he was a source of trouble. John had agreed. Angry as it made Peter, he knew it was true. He was always putting his foot into a mess, then having to sit down and laboriously wipe it off.

Jesus turned to face them. "But who do you say that I am?"

An explosive question. An answer to up-end the world.

The disciples looked at each other, unwilling to speak, but Peter knew the answer. He felt it in his belly, down to his toes. He could almost grip it in his two hands. He had always known it.

"You are the Messiah," he blurted out. "The Son of the living God." The others stared. For one instant Peter was appalled at his presumption. The next instant, Jesus laughed.

"Blessed are you, Simon bar Jonah! Flesh and blood have not revealed this to you, but my Father in heaven." He pulled Peter to his feet, putting his big carpenter's hands on Peter's shoulders. "I tell you, you are Peter. On this rock I will build my church, and the gates of hell will not prevail against it!"

Peter stared at him, dumbfounded.

"I will give you the keys of the kingdom of heaven," said Jesus. "Whatever you bind on earth will be bound in heaven. Whatever you loose on earth will be loosed in heaven."

It was magnificent. It was shocking. He was exalted. He was *not ready*.

"Master!" It was Zacchaeus, hailing them from the road above. The enthusiastic little fellow had become the leader of the other disciples on this trip. He was always needing to speak with the Master.

Peter groaned—he had so many questions! How was he to begin to fathom these things?

Jesus squeezed his shoulder. "We'll talk tonight."

But that night there was no time. John and James took Peter aside to ask his understanding of one of Jesus' parables. And his brother Andrew was busy telling childhood stories of Peter to Miriam of Magdala. Andrew looked at Peter now and again with a new expression in his eyes—as if Peter had grown suddenly taller in the space of six hours. It began to worry Peter.

The next day was just as harried. The growing size of the party didn't help. Five days ago, they had stopped to see Miriam of Magdala on their way north. The sisters from Bethany were staying with her. After talking to Jesus, Miriam of Magdala, Martha and Miriam of Bethany, and nine other followers asked to come with them. Now they were a caravan of thirty, with donkeys carrying food and water, and pots banging as they walked.

Peter was tired and feeling glum. They had walked seventeen miles today. Jesus strode ahead, silent and driven again, like a saiboat running before a strong wind. Ever since the Baptist's death he'd been this way, focused on some distant, urgent task of which he said nothing. In late afternoon, Jesus led the Twelve down to refill their water skins from the Jordan. It was warmer in the valley out of the wind. Jesus sat down and drew with a stick in the crusted sand.

"My friends," he said, "I must go to Jerusalem."

The hair on the back of Peter's neck rose. Trouble for sure, perhaps even danger. The elders, priests, and scribes were arrayed against Jesus like a Roman Legion.

John nudged Peter. "Say something. Tell him he must not do this."

There it was again; he was the leader, the spokesman. He cleared his throat. "Wouldn't it be better to stay away for now?"

Jesus looked up at Peter. His brown eyes seemed like deep water in shadow, their light eclipsed.

Jesus seemed to weigh each word separately. "I am destined to go to Jerusalem," he said slowly. "I will suffer there at the hands of the elders and priests and scribes. I will be put to death—"

"No!" Peter cried.

"—and I will be raised up on the third day."

"What?" said Nathanael.

Thaddaeus stuttered, "Wh-when will this happen, Lord?"

"Will this help our cause?" That was Judas.

John said, "But if you are the Messiah, can't you—"

Jesus held up a hand. "Let it be for now. But speak of these things to no one." He climbed the hill ahead of them, embraced by the women as he moved through them to the road.

A rough wind sprang up from the west, driving sand and grit into their eyes. The disciples walked at the rear, talking in low voices. Peter lagged at the very end. He longed to be in the Temple in Jerusalem, to throw himself down before the Most High and beg for Jesus' life. He tightened his cloak against the wind and began to pray.

Most High, how can this be your will for Jesus? Look at us! We would be like sheep without a shepherd if he dies. We need him. Your people need him. Please—let this not come to pass! He longed for assurance, for an answer, but there was none. Was it possible that this future horror was the will of God? Was he gainsaying the will of the Most High? No, it was impossible! This could not be God's plan!

John and James dropped back to him. "This is a calamity!" rasped James. "How can the Master speak of such a thing? The others hesitate to speak, but I say we must stop him."

John gripped Peter's arm. "Speak for us, Peter! Talk to Jesus. Make him change his mind!"

Peter groaned in distress. Was *this* a sign, a confirmation from the Holy One? It was what he wanted to say. It must be right. He walked ahead. The Master was talking with Martha and Miriam. Peter tried to stay back, to wait patiently, but urgent, fearful words rattled through his brain.

"Lord, I must speak with you!" His words came out louder than he expected.

The sisters turned to look at him. Martha's eyes snapped a little. She was a solid, robust woman, always planning for the Master's needs. So different from her quiet, slender sister.

"Master—" Martha said.

Jesus put a hand on her arm and said, "There will be time." The women dropped back.

"Master, I must speak to you about—what you said to us."

"Peter." Jesus' single word was a sentence, a restraint.

Peter looked over at him. The wind sent the hair streaming back from the Master's head. There was anguish etched in Jesus' face, around his eyes, across his forehead, as if a cruel hand had carved it there with a knife.

Peter gripped Jesus' arm. "God forbid!" he shouted. "God forbid that such a thing should happen to you, Lord!"

Jesus halted and, with a jerk, he threw off Peter's hand. "Get behind me, Satan!" he cried. "You are an *obstacle* to me!"

Suddenly nothing, Peter knelt in the dust. Everyone halted. All eyes were on them. Peter covered his mouth with his hand, wishing God would strike him dumb.

"You think not as God does, but as people do!" said Jesus.

"I want—to protect you," Peter whispered.

He saw Jesus close his eyes. The wind died. Earth seemed to sway to a stop. Jesus put down a hand and pulled Peter to his feet. He looked directly into Peter's eyes.

"Brother," whispered Jesus, "if you wish to come after me, you must deny yourself. Take up your cross. Follow me."

Late that night, Peter lay awake in the dark. His hip was aching—from the walking, he supposed. He turned over, but he couldn't stretch out his legs. Jesus was off praying in the mountains. The men were packed together in one room, the women in the other. *Like fish laid out for market,* Peter thought. He should be grateful that this man Gideon had given them his hospitality. At least they weren't sleeping outside.

Someone began to whisper at the far side. Someone else answered. Peter tried to ignore the sound, but it was like a cricket clacking in the corner. The voices grew louder. No doubt they thought everyone was asleep.

"I think so," said one voice clearly.

"Will Jesus name another leader?" asked the other. Peter opened his eyes and stared at Bartholomew's back.

"He might, after what happened today." It was John talking to James—about him. With a grunt, Peter threw off his blanket and got to his feet. Sudden silence from them. Peter stepped between the sleepers to the doorway.

The air outside was cold, the wind high. Peter stumped across the courtyard, found wood, and built himself a little fire. He sat before it and rubbed his hands, angry but satisfied. At least here he could be alone. After a time, he heard the door open. He hunched his shoulders, hoping it was someone coming out to relieve himself. The footsteps faded, then returned.

"You act like a man afflicted with a boil." It was Martha standing on the far side of the fire, her arms crossed.

"Go away," said Peter.

"No." She sat on a log at the far side of the fire. She must, he decided, be one of those women who liked to argue for the sheer exercise of it. She was forever fixing things, weaving Jesus a cloak, baking bread for his journeys. Perhaps she thought she could fix him, too.

"The others are talking about the way the Master chastised you," she said. Peter poked in the fire with a stick. "The Master has chastised me, too, you know."

Peter glowered at her. "That's different."

Her chin went up. "Why? We are all his followers."

"Because Jesus expects me to lead. At least, that's what he told me two days ago." Peter's voice began to shake. "But I didn't lead. I did something terrible. I—injured him somehow."

She tucked her skirts in around her legs. "What? You think the Master no longer loves you? That he can't forgive you?"

"It's not a matter of forgiving me!" shouted Peter. "Everything is confusing now! Everything has changed. It's—" He waved his hands helplessly. "I'm a fisherman, good for nothing but pulling in the nets. I don't understand the Master's words or his plans." He halted. He must come no nearer to Jesus' prophecy.

He looked at her. "Does the Lord speak of his plans—to you?" He'd always been curious about what Jesus said to the women. All those hours of talking in private when the Twelve weren't present.

"He rests with us. He shares his heart," she said, but her eyes held a mischievous spark. "As to his plans, they're not all *that* hard to understand." Peter had an angry retort on his lips. Martha seemed to relent. "All right. Tell me, was it easier in the beginning?"

Peter stared at the fire for a moment. "It seems long ago now. I remember that morning when he came to the Sea of Galilee. He asked to use our boat to speak to the crowd. I noticed while he talked that shoals of fish surrounded our boat as if they were a herd of sheep. And the people. They came to him hungry, and he fed them—with bread, stories, with himself."

He looked up at her. "Afterward, he told us to put down the nets, and every fish in the sea rushed to our puny little boat! I had to call James and John and Zebedee to help us. The nets nearly ripped with the weight of that catch!" He wiped a hand across his eyes. "Everything was simple then. He taught people. He loved them. He healed them."

Martha nodded. "Our first meeting was simple, too. I was in synagogue one Sabbath when he preached. I was thinking about fixing supper, when Miriam gripped my arm and whispered, 'Listen!'"

"What did he say?" asked Peter.

Martha quoted Isaiah from memory. "'O afflicted one, storm-tossed and not comforted! I will set your stones in antimony, and lay your foundations with sapphires. . . . Your children shall be taught by the Lord, and great shall be the prosperity of your children.'" She said, "I felt the Master speaking to me directly, to all I had lost."

"What do you mean?" said Peter.

Martha said, "I have borne four children. They all died before they had lived a month."

Peter stared at her dumbly. How old was she? Twenty-eight?

"Now I am a widow and not likely to marry again, for what man wants to marry a woman whose babies die?" Her mouth curved down a moment. "As we left the synagogue, Jesus stopped before us and asked to come to eat—as if he knew us. Lazarus was put off, but Miriam said yes. The Lord became our friend. And gradually I found a home."

Peter lifted his eyebrows.

Martha said, "Oh, in one way, it's nothing new. Our same house in Bethany. But I began to help women with birthing, and to feed the beggars who pass through Bethany on their way to Jerusalem. It may seem a small thing, but it is not. I am—" She paused. "—contented. But I do agree with you. Everything for him is changing."

Peter shook his head. "It began with the Baptist's death. Now he talks of seed sown on stony ground; he foretells persecution. He calls the leaders a brood of vipers. Now they watch his every step, waiting for their chance. I am afraid for him."

"And so you spoke to him today," she said.

"Yes."

"My sister and I are also worried. Miriam took one look at him in Magdala and said we had to change our plans, though we've had word that Lazarus is ill at home. I'm often impatient with Miriam's impulses. They're impractical, I tell her. But this time, she's right. The Master looks parched inside."

That was it exactly. With growing respect, Peter looked at her. "But why are you smiling?" he asked.

She stretched her legs in front of her. "For many days, it has been in my mind that this—this storm gathering over him is like something else. I've been trying and trying to think what it is. Now I know."

"What?" said Peter.

"It's like waiting for a baby to be born."

Peter stared hard. He saw her lips curve into a sly smile.

"Your eyes will stay crossed if you keep doing that."

Exasperated, he laughed. "For what are you talking about babies, Martha?"

"No, listen!" she said. "A change is coming. I feel it. Like when a baby is coming to be born." She clasped her hands together. "I wish husbands could be with their wives when the babies come. Then maybe they'd understand."

"What's to understand?" said Peter.

Martha's eyes were intent on the fire. "You wait and wait for that baby. You take joy in it growing inside you. But in the back of your mind, you know you will face agony. And not only that; so many women, so many babies die. You must risk everything."

"You mean," said Peter, "that Jesus is risking this?"

She nodded. "And when the time comes, you work and sweat and plead with the Most High for relief, but there is none. It takes hours, days. You have no control. Your heart seems to break wide open. You surrender." She stopped. When she went on, her voice was softer. "Then you give birth. Light breaks around you. You hold new life in your arms. There's nothing dearer in the world."

"But what if the agony is terrible?" Peter whispered. "What if it's worse than anything you can imagine?"

Martha gazed at him over the fire. "The Master is taking that risk for the sake of what will come. I am his friend. I must be ready to take it with him. Are you?"

✦ ✦ ✦

As the Gospels tell, a few days later, Peter denied he even knew this man he had loved and followed for three years. Yet Peter's genuine humility saved him. Whenever Peter

sinned, he crawled back to Christ again, con-
fident of Jesus' love. After Pentecost, Peter
would become the leader of the new church,
and then the first bishop of Rome, though he
had to be corrected again and again by God,
by the Apostles and Paul.

There is a legend told of Peter in his old
age. He leaves Rome, knowing that the Ro-
mans plan to kill him. He meets Jesus walking
in the other direction. Peter prostrates himself before the Lord and asks where he is going. "To Rome, to be crucified again," comes
the reply. At that, Peter turns and goes back
to face martyrdom.

Holy Boy

Patrick

Patrick, or Patricius as he was called in his time, was born around A.D. 390 to educated Romanized Britons, probably in western Britain. His father, Calpornius, was a church deacon, his grandfather a priest. At the age of fifteen, just beginning his higher education in rhetoric and writing, Patricius was captured by Irish pirates and enslaved in western or northern Ireland, where he herded sheep.

✦ ✦ ✦

Patricius stood with his back against a rock, talking. The sound of his prayer seemed to calm the herds below him in the mist. He knew it calmed him.

"Ho, there!"

He was so startled he didn't answer at first. It had been many days since he'd heard another human voice.

"Patricius!" The voice was closer, but it was hard to tell where it was coming from.

"I am here," Patricius called uncertainly. He scanned the hillside, but he could see only ten feet beyond him. Then the mist shifted, and brown-headed Donal, Milliucc's twelve-year-old grandson, came into sight, leading a pony. Behind him tramped Adalbert the slave, sour as usual.

Patricius formed his words slowly. "You are far from home."

"Someone had to fetch you," said Donal. "I thought it might as well be me. I didn't realize I'd have him along in the bargain." He gestured back to Adalbert. Patricius almost allowed a smile to his lips. No doubt Donal had thought he'd have a fine solitary gallop over the hills.

"You're to come back to the hill-fort," said Donal. "Grandfather has need of you. Adalbert will stay in your stead."

Patricius led them to his hut of stones and branches. He showed Adalbert the food supplies and rabbit traps, gave him directions to firewood and to the stream.

"You can bathe there, too," he said before he thought.

Adalbert scratched the crusted mud on his fleshy arms and laughed. "Just like a Roman, always thinking about his next bath."

Patricius said, "Your flock numbers eighty-four. Two of the ewes are ailing. I've marked their backs with mud." He handed the shepherd's crook to Adalbert. "You'll need this. The lambs can wander off and get caught in the clefts." The man hardly seemed to be listening. Patricius wondered how he would care for the sheep. Adalbert usually worked in the iron forge. *The hired man abandons the sheep as soon as he sees the wolf coming.* That slip of Scripture seemed to fit.

Patricius went in the shelter. He tucked the cross he'd formed from twigs into the rope at his waist. Then he picked up his rabbit-fur cloak and fought briefly with himself. He would be cold without it, but Adalbert would be colder yet up here in the hills. With a sigh, he left it and picked up his staff.

"When will he come back?" Adalbert said to Donal.

"I don't know."

Only five sheep were visible in the mist. The valley was lonely and strange, without even the song of a bird. Adalbert stared around him.

"It's like being locked in a small, clammy room," Patricius said. "But it will break soon."

Adalbert didn't answer, but Patricius saw his face change. Adalbert needed to say something, but it was utterly beyond his powers of speech. Then comprehension rose in Patricius's mind like a bubble rising through dark water. Adalbert knew the Irish tales of the in-between places, neither day nor night, neither sun nor storm, where shape-shifters appeared. Did he hold to the Irish gods—good Dagda, Lug the skilled, and the dreadful Morrigan? Or did he believe in tree spirits from his home in far-off Europe? No matter; Adalbert was afraid.

"God is here," said Patricius. "You are protected."

At that, Adalbert spat noisily at Patricius's feet. "Get away from me, holy boy."

Patricius ran after Donal on his pony over the hill and down into the valley, warmed by the exercise. After a time, the cow path gleamed. A lark began to sing; the moss on the trees glowed green. Then, as if light were filtered between the fingers of a giant hand, separate rays of sunlight poured into the valley.

Patricius's heart lifted. Adalbert would be less afraid now. *Oh, Jerusalem, how I have longed to gather you as a hen gathers her chicks under her wings, but you would not.* Adalbert needed the mercy of God in the wild hills. God would be present to Adalbert, he was sure of it, whether Adalbert liked it or not.

And he? He had recalled more Holy Scripture. For months he had trained himself as he watched the sheep to remember his home church in Bannavem Taberniae. He became again a disinterested ten-year-old at Mass, his nose running from the musty smell, the gray daylight barely penetrating between the pillars. His mind had run to games and adventures then, not to Holy Scripture. But now, if he patiently centered himself in the memory and waited, the jewels of Scripture were his reward.

At the top of the next sunny hill was a green tomb mound. Donal seemed to hold his breath as he and Patricius passed the yawning stone entrance. Patricius had seen many tomb mounds in his first journey across Ireland. They were ancient places. Irish druid priests sometimes went there for their rites, but it seemed to Patricius that even they did not fully know the mounds' purpose, though they claimed their power.

Beyond the mound, Donal shook himself and said, "Don't you want to know why Grandfather wants you back?"

"I do. Why has he called me?"

Donal's cheeks flamed with excitement. "Niall and the others are home from the raid in Britain. They brought good booty—bars of silver, jewels, and coins. And slaves, of course."

Patricius took a breath and halted. *Slaves. Bereft of all.*

". . . and a big wooden trunk," Donal was saying. He turned back. "Why did you stop?"

Patricius forced himself forward.

Donal said, "In the trunk were those co—, codi—those boxy things with marks inside."

Patricius's heart jumped. "Codices? Books?!" He had not held a book in his hands since he was captured.

"Yes!" said Donal triumphantly. "I told Grandfather you're the only slave who can read. Tonight at the feast, you're to tell us what they say. And here's a perfect secret." He leaned close and whispered, "You can teach me to read."

Patricius stared up into Donal's blue eyes. "You want to learn Latin?"

Donal's chin jutted out. "Why not? I'm smart enough!"

"Of course you are," said Patricius. Donal in fact drove his mother to distraction with his curiosity. When Patricius had first come to the hill-fort, Donal had peppered him with questions about life in Britain. They were agony to answer in those first months of his capture. Yet the boy seemed to yearn for anything that was just out of sight of his own place. Patricius had not had the heart to force him away.

"I'll teach you," he said, "if Milliucc agrees."

"Oh, Grandfather will. It's the best way to shut me up," said Donal, and Patricius laughed.

Donal said, "I think Adalbert was afraid to be left alone back there. Are you ever afraid in the hills?"

"I was at first," said Patricius. He remembered the sting of rain on his naked back, how he had lain down amid the herds, desperate for warmth, crying out his family's names. He was constantly hungry; he'd been given only moldy bread and parsnips to eat. He'd lived like a wounded animal, blind to anything except getting through the next excruciating moment, wishing for death, terrified of it, begging for help from he knew not where.

And help had come. Not what he begged for; no soldiers from Britain appeared miraculously at the hilltop to rescue him. Instead, he awoke to a potent voice singing on the edge of sleep. The next day he felt a surprising strength when wild hounds attacked the herds. Then the vivid, ample voice declared itself in his mind, and a presence radiated around him, so palpable that he sometimes felt a loving hand on his head. He was a baptized Christian, yet he discovered the word slowly. *God*. Gradually he'd awakened to spring, to the birds, rabbits, and foxes. He devised clumsy traps using the guts of a dead ewe and caught game. He sewed a cloak of rabbit skin, and he repaired the ruined shepherd's hut.

"Patricius, aren't you listening?" Donal sounded riled.

Patricius started. "Excuse me."

"I said, 'You're not afraid, are you?'"

"No, not often."

"Is it because of your god that you're not afraid? But which god? Dagda or Lug?"

"The one true God, the only God, Father, Son, and Spirit."

"You think there's only one God and no other?"

"There is only one," said Patricius. "God created us, he redeemed us, he loves us."

"A god who loves? What a strange idea."

"God's love is all-powerful. How could God not love us? Look! He created all this for us." Patricius lifted his arms to display the green hills drenched with sunlight and the radiant sky.

Donal laughed. "It's Ireland," he said, as if that explained everything.

The earthen walls of Milliucc's hill-fort rose above the Wood of Voclut. As they climbed, Patricius could hear voices, horses stamping, the clang of metal. Inside the gate, his chest constricted and he halted. More than twenty slaves stood in the yard. Linked by iron chains, their wrists bleeding, they looked as miserable as beaten dogs. The men were naked. The women held their ragged clothes carefully to cover themselves. Patricius looked down; his own wrists still bore scars from those links.

He studied their wan faces and sunken eyes. Likely they hadn't been fed or given water in days. For an instant, he tasted again on his tongue the metallic tang of extreme thirst. He looked around. Donal had gone into the stable. The masters were greeting chieftains on the other side of the fort; perhaps no one would notice.

He fetched water from the trough for them, stopped at the head of the line and said in a low voice, "One at a time. Aqua."

The slaves' eyes widened; they lifted their heads. Patricius held the pitcher, right, left, right, left, as they drank. At the end, a giant of a man grabbed it; water ran down his hairy chest in his eagerness. Then behind him, two small, trembling hands were raised.

Mercy, thought Patricius, *children*. They were brown-haired, filthy, their tattered clothes smelling of vomit. They'd had a rough sea crossing, then. He lifted the pitcher. The girl drank. The boy was of the same height, the same look. They were twins.

"How old?" Patricius whispered.

The boy wiped his mouth carefully. "Ten years."

"Your names?"

"Lucius and Julia," said the boy.

"What's this?" bellowed a voice. "Who told you to water the slaves?" Rebachan, Milliucc's brother, pushed his way through the slaves. He was a mean man, with a face seared by frustration at being brother and not king. Patricius saw the blow coming. He staggered under its force.

"That'll teach you," said Rebachan. "Now slaves, time for the king to decide your price." He grabbed the links of the slaves in front and yanked. Like a row of dolls, the slaves fell forward.

When they were gone, Patricius wiped the blood from his lip and set the pitcher on its hook. The slaves would be sold tonight. They would be starved and mistreated; the females would be raped. They were forever lost to family and home. As he was. *I am a worm and not a man.* Where did that bit of Scripture come from? No matter. The one who wrote it knew slavery.

The feast was well under way when he arrived. In the center, fire bloomed like a hot yellow rose. The great round room was thick with the smell of sweat and the fragrance of venison. Patricius's stomach rumbled; his own meager meal of bread and cabbage had been hours ago. Roman wine from the raid was passed from table to table; the crowd grew raucous.

He found the slaves crouched against the wall. Some of them had been thrown castoffs from the meal. The big slave had a hoard of bones between his crossed legs; he snapped them in two to dig out the marrow. The children sat behind him. They had no food. The girl was unmoving, her face dull. Her brother had his arm around her shoulder, his eyes dark and hungry.

I must find them a morsel, Patricius thought. Donal sat nearby with his mother, Moriath. Donal was watching him narrowly, and Patricius had an uncomfortable feeling Donal knew he was thinking about food for the slaves.

"Patricius!" Milliucc roared like a bugling elk. The room grew silent. He stood up. The heavy gold torc around Milliucc's neck and the gold rings on his arms glowed in the firelight.

"I am here," said Patricius.

"Bring out the trunk!" Milliucc ordered. Two codices were lifted out, and Patricius's heart began to pound. The treasures of civilization—Roman rhetoric, Greek philosophy, mathematics, history. Who knew what these might be? He picked up the larger codex first, then his heart sank. The cover was damp; it crumbled in his hand. He touched the bottom of the trunk. The wood was spongy. The trunk had sat in seawater.

"Tell us what it says," said Milliucc.

Patricius opened the cover. The vellum sent up a stench of mildew. He sneezed.

Rebachan laughed. "I can smell Roman rot even from here."

The poems of Virgil. He had begun to study Virgil just days before he was captured. He tried to turn the pages, but each was glued to the next in one sticky mass.

"Well?" said Milliucc.

Sick with disappointment, Patricius said, "This one is ruined, Master." He picked up the next book. It was smaller, not as well made, but not so damp, either. He opened it, then he almost let out a shout. *Second Epistle to the Corinthians.*

He gaped in wonder at the faces around him. Donal sat straight and intense, staring at him. Milliucc studied him, as did the visiting chieftains. Rebachan looked surly. Patricius was stricken with a sudden, inarticulate longing toward them all. He held in his hands words mighty enough to alter this world, to reshape lives, from Milliucc to the most miserable slave. If these words were preached with power, these people could seize the everlasting kingdom—but how to begin?

"Well?" said Milliucc impatiently.

With shaking fingers, Patricius turned the pages. Then slowly, so he would not stumble over the unfamiliar Latin, he translated. "We are in difficulties on all sides, but never cornered. We see no answer to our problems, but never despair; we have been persecuted, but never deserted; knocked down, but never killed; always, wherever we may be, we carry with us in our body the death of Jesus, so that the life of Jesus, too, may be openly shown. So death is at work in us, but life in you—"

The codex was yanked out of his hands. Rebachan leaned close to him, his eyes bleary with drink. "We don't need your Christian books, slave. We have our own ways here, our own gods." He swayed a little. "I say we get rid of these stinking things right now." Rebachan flung both books into the fire.

Patricius stood frozen in agony.

"No!" cried Donal, and he sprinted toward the fire.

"Donal!" called his mother.

With a guffaw, Rebachan caught Donal and held him while everyone laughed. Donal fought him silently. Patricius stared at the books. Oily black smoke began to coil up from them as the flame reached the damp vellum. Then Donal stopped fighting. Rebachan let him go, and Donal stumbled back to his seat. Rebachan slumped down on the bench. Milliucc shrugged and sat down.

Patricius turned away in near despair. He had no power here. He was a slave. He would always be a slave. And he might never again hold the Scriptures in his hand.

But as he passed Donal's table, the boy grabbed his arm. He held Patricius there, looking up at him with furious, rebellious eyes. Patricius covered Donal's hand with his own in silent sympathy. Still holding on, Donal reached for a haunch of venison. He took a bite, looked up at Patricius and lowered the meat below the table. Patricius heard a soft thump as it hit the floor. Then Donal dumped his mug of water across the table.

"Aaugh! Patricius! Clean this up!" he cried.

His mother turned around. "Clean it yourself, clumsy boy!"

"But he's standing right here!" protested Donal.

She glanced up. "All right, then."

Patricius mopped the table with a rag. He mopped the floor and rolled the meat into the cloth. It was pitifully little, but this he could do. Patricius sat down in front of the children and put both hands behind his back. In his left hand was the meat in the rag, in the right, his cross of twigs.

"Bring up the first slave!" roared Milliucc.

✦ ✦ ✦

After six years of captivity, Patricius was guided by a dream to escape. He walked two hundred miles to the coast, found a ship, and returned home. He trained for the priesthood. Home again, he dreamed of an Irishman bearing letters with the heading, "The voice of the Irish." Their many voices cried, "Holy boy, we ask you to come and walk among us again." Around A.D. 432, Patricius returned to northern Ireland as missionary bishop. There he converted thousands, ordained priests, and founded monasteries.

Many enchanting stories are told of Patricius, but most were first circulated three hundred years after his death. Patricius left only two writings. *The Epistle to Coroticus* was written to a Scottish Christian chieftain who had enslaved Patricius's newly baptized Christians. Outraged, Patricius excommunicated Coroticus and his men until the slaves were freed. He also wrote his *Confession* to defend against attacks on his character. There he gives the biographical facts used in the above fictional story.

Patricius was sublimely certain of God's calling for his life. "I was like a stone that lies in deep mud," he wrote. "He who is mighty came and in his compassion raised me up and . . . placed me on the top of the wall." By the time of Patricius's death around A.D. 450–475, slavery was abolished in Ireland.

When Heward Jumped Down from the Wall

Boniface

Born in A.D. 675, Boniface was an English Benedictine who evangelized what is now Germany and the Netherlands. Much like circuit riders in the American West, he walked or rode thousands of miles through wilderness, preaching, baptizing, building churches, and advising chieftains and kings.

Boniface was a genius at calling forth the best from people. He coaxed many English Benedictines to follow him into the field for, he said, "We are bound in blood and bone to these people." Their ancestry was so close, in fact, that the English spoke a common language with the German Saxons.

At the age of seventy-eight, after thirty-four years in Germany, Boniface resigned his archbishopric and went to Friesland, the low-lying coast west of Jutland in what is now the Netherlands. As a young man, he had twice preached there unsuccessfully. Knowing that his time was short, he returned to try again.

✦ ✦ ✦

Heward worked doggedly shoring up the dike. For weeks he had moved dirt and built walls, and then he had to do the job all over again after it rained. He was exhausted, but it didn't matter; the North Sea would flood soon. The gray clouds above him were many-layered and delicate, shaped like the scales of a fish. More rain coming. He drove his shovel into the ground. Four years ago this spring, Mother and Grandfather had been swept away by a flood as they tried to rescue the cows.

The North Sea gave the Frieslanders herring. It allowed pastures for cattle and sheep. The sea was the clan's source, their toil, their companion. And it was their constant fear. Would the dikes hold back the next flood? How many huts would be destroyed? How many cattle lost? How many would die?

"Sea and Sky, Sky and Sea . . ." Heward sang the charm, hardly aware he spoke aloud. People of the clan often sang it as they worked. Some years, it seemed, its power held them safe.

"Heward!"

He jumped and whirled around. Grandmother stood at the top of the dike, her hands on her hips.

"Grandmother," he protested, "everyone else does it! There's no harm to it. You can pray to Jesus, too."

Grandmother stalked across the top of the dike. He gave her a hand to climb down. Eight inches shorter than he, she still managed to look imposing.

"Kneel," she said. Heward knelt. Grunting, she sank to her knees beside him. "Now, repeat the sayings."

Heward clenched his teeth. Grandmother didn't understand anything! She hardly let him finish a sentence, let alone ask questions about this God that she wanted him to follow.

She batted his arm.

"Jesus ate with sinners and outcasts," he muttered.

"Blessed are the poor and humble," she said.

"If you have faith like a tiny seed," he said, "I don't understand that one—"

"Sh!" she hissed. "Jesus calmed the raging waters."

"Lilies do not toil or spin."

Grandmother paused, her next words quiet. "My body is given for you. Remember me." Heward started to rise, but her hand held him in place. "One God, please forgive this foolish Heward. He doesn't understand."

"Grandmother—"

"Save us from wind and flood and storm. Protect our people, even those who scorn you. Have mercy on us."

"Amen," said Heward. He walked home with questions roiling hotly in his head. *If the one God is so powerful, why are we the only ones in the clan who follow him? Our enemies, the Franks, follow this God. How could their God ever be Friesland's God, too?* And the worst question. *Why did God let Mother and Grandfather die?*

As they reached the hut, they heard the rumble of horses' hooves. Grandmother peered into the distance, and Heward saw her face brighten a moment.

"Strangers," she said.

"A large party," said Heward. He grasped his shovel.

"Put that down!" said Grandmother. "We welcome them."

"I'm just holding it," he said.

She threw him a reproachful look before she went inside the hut, as tradition required. Heward did his best to look steady and unafraid. He was nearly seventeen, after all. Soon twenty riders with packhorses came into view. They halted before him.

"Welcome," Heward said stiffly. Greeting strangers had long been an act of honor in the clan; it showed the welcomer to be both brave and generous. But now? Heward knew that Haakon, his clan's chieftain, would be furious that he had offered even this one grudging word. Since the last battle with the Franks, Haakon thought every stranger was a Frankish spy; his fear infected the whole village. But Grandmother insisted that they give strangers food and shelter, because it was custom and because Jesus commanded it.

Heward noticed few weapons among the strangers. They must be rich since they rode horses, but they were dressed simply. Five of them wore the same dark robes. Two in front got down. The first man was solid and short with dark hair going gray. The other was an old man, bald, with blue eyes and a wide-seeing, unguarded look. An elder, thought Heward, and due respect.

"We have grown unaccustomed to welcome," said the old man.

He had an unfamiliar accent, but Heward understood him. Heward tossed his head in the direction of the village. "You may not find those ahead so friendly. People are afraid of strangers now."

"Ah," said the old man, "because they might be Franks?"

Heward nodded.

"Be reassured, we are not your enemies. We come from Frankish lands far to the south, but we are not Franks ourselves."

Heward bowed and said the traditional words. "We are honored that you rest here."

The elder smiled. "Thank you."

Heward showed them a spot to make camp. They began stringing shelters between the high bushes. Heward went to the hut. Grandmother was squatting beside a large pot of water on the peat fire, cutting up salted herring.

Heward couldn't help himself. "That's the last of our herring. Who will feed us when the strangers have gone?"

"God, of course," she said, without looking up.

Heward sighed. It wasn't worth arguing. Grandmother was his only family. He did his best to honor her, but it was hard. Did he love her? The question seemed to catch inside him. He didn't know for sure. Grandmother had been kinder and happier before the flood. The last time Haakon had come to buy her weaving, she'd given him a thorough tongue-lashing about villagers driving off strangers. She hardly exchanged a word with the village wives anymore. Even Heward's dike repair showed the rift; not one clansman came to help.

An hour later Heward lugged the heavy soup pot to the strangers' camp; Grandmother carried their few bowls. The elder gripped the handle of the cauldron to help Heward. Together they set it down in the fire.

"I am Boniface," the old man said. He pointed to the dark-haired man. "This is Eoban. And these are Wintung, Walteri, Ethelheri, Waccar and Gundwaccar . . ."

"This is my grandmother, Bertilla. I am Heward, of the clan Haakonii of Friesland."

"We are grateful for your hospitality, Bertilla and Heward."

Grandmother said apologetically, "We have only three bowls."

"We have bowls and spoons with us," said Eoban. These were produced and the soup ladled into them.

Heward had lifted the first spoonful to his mouth when Boniface said, "It is right to pray before we eat."

Irked, Heward put down the spoon. That was the thing about strangers. One never knew what their gods or customs would be. Boniface had closed his eyes, so Heward did, too.

"We give thanks for this gift of food, and for these good people. Keep us all safe. May your Son, Jesus—"

Grandmother let out a cry. Her bowl clattered to the ground. Everyone jumped. Grandmother was staring wide-eyed at Boniface.

"Christian?" she croaked.

Light came up in the old man's face. "Yes!"

Grandmother put her hands to her cheeks, unable to speak.

"Grandmother is Christian," blurted Heward.

With cries of pleasure, the men gathered around her. Boniface embraced her, led her to a rock, and sat her down.

"My sister in Christ, who was your teacher? How long ago were you converted?"

"A holy man," she began, "named Willibrord—"

"Ah! My old teacher!" exclaimed Boniface.

Heward saw Grandmother's eyes widen. "You knew him?"

"He was my teacher many years ago when I first came as missionary to Friesland."

Tears began to roll down Grandmother's face. Heward was shocked; he had seen her cry only once before, when Mother and Grandfather died. He wanted to comfort her, but he was overcome with the strangeness of the situation.

Grandmother whispered, "I thought no one remembered Willibrord except me."

Boniface said, "Willibrord is the father of our missions here. We remember him with love and gratitude." Boniface squeezed her hand. "You have been alone a long time, Bertilla."

"Thirty-two years."

Eoban said, "How did you keep your faith alive without Holy Scripture, without the Mass?"

"My husband and daughter believed . . ." said Grandmother.

"But they died four years ago," put in Heward.

"Five, maybe six times, Christian travelers came to the village. Some of them were Franks, some not. I talked to them, asked them what they knew. But then the Franks attacked us and travelers stopped coming this way." Her voice became a whisper. "So I prayed."

For as long as Heward could remember, Grandmother prayed every day, outside if the weather was good. Grandfather had built her a lean-to on the beach. After the flood, she'd made Heward rebuild it before he started the shed for the animals. He had been cranky about it, he remembered. Sometimes at night, he woke to hear her murmuring, but not to him. In the first months after the flood, he had found her soft words strangely comforting.

Next afternoon, Heward was back at work, mulling over the strangers. He looked up and saw the old man standing above him.

"You've been working hard," Boniface said. "You need rest."

"Rest?" Heward straightened painfully. "No one rests in the spring. The dikes must be repaired."

"Our men will help you later. Come, let's talk. We'll take the horses."

The lure of a horse was too much; Heward rarely got a chance to ride. Only Haakon and three others in the village had them. Boniface led them at an easy pace down to a sheltered beach. He dismounted, spread his cloak on the sand, and sat down.

"It is good to be back," he said, watching the gray waves.

Heward looked at him in surprise. "Most strangers to Friesland can't wait to leave. They say it's flat and boring."

Boniface lifted his face to the thin sunlight. "It is not readily lovely like the mountains, but there is a wideness, a power here, don't you think? Look at that enormous sky, and the clouds like fleets of ships advancing to the shore."

Heward shrugged. "I'd rather live where there are trees. I'm tired of cutting peat for the fire."

Boniface was silent awhile, then he said, "Your family is Christian. It must be difficult for you if your village is not."

"Grandmother is Christian. I'm not," Heward said defiantly.

Boniface studied him. "Are you pagan, then?"

People in the village would call Heward a liar if he said yes. He shook his head. "I'm neither."

"Ah, you do not believe wholly in Woden and the Norse gods, nor in Christ." The old man said it as a fact, not a judgment.

Heward said, "Before the flood, I believed, but not after Mother and Grandfather died. Our hut was destroyed. All we had left was my shovel and Grandmother's loom. I found the loom perched on a rock at low tide. Grandmother said it was a miracle it survived."

"Did you think it was a miracle?" asked Boniface.

Heward darted a look at the old man. "It would have been a miracle if Mother and Grandfather lived."

Boniface touched Heward's arm. "You've had a terrible loss. I'm sorry."

Heward's throat tightened. "The clan turned against us after that, even my friends. They say Woden cursed us for refusing to worship at the great oak." He pushed his fist into the sand. "And now that you're here, Grandmother will want me to be baptized."

"Do you wish to be baptized?" Boniface asked.

"I just want to be left alone!" blurted Heward.

"I can see why. You're perched on a wall between your grandmother and the clan. Either way you jump, you lose."

What Boniface said was bitterly true. And here he had been expecting the old man to pressure him to be baptized.

"That makes it all the harder for you to understand your grandmother, to see how she is preoccupied by her own hunger."

Heward stared at him. "What d'you mean? We eat well enough most of the time."

"Not that kind of hunger, my son," said Boniface. "Faith is meant to be lived out in community. We support each other, pray together, celebrate Eucharist together. Bertilla had only your mother and grandfather, then she lost them." He shook his head. "She is like John the Baptist."

"Who's he?" Heward asked.

"Another who followed God alone. John lived a long time in a desert. When he came back to his people, it seemed his main occupation was to make them uncomfortable."

Heward couldn't help himself. He laughed.

A smile lit the old man's face. "I am right, then?"

"Haakon, our chieftain, says Grandmother's like a fly buzzing around his head. Most of the clan agrees with him. Grandmother is so sure of herself that she overrules any other possibility. I think the only reason Haakon doesn't drive us away completely is Grandmother's weaving. She's the best weaver in the village. Her cloth is guaranteed to sell to southern traders."

Boniface shook his head. "Such obstacles, and yet your grandmother has lived all these years by prayer." His voice cracked suddenly. "It is Christ himself who sustains her."

Christ was sustaining Grandmother? What exactly did that mean?

Boniface stood and dusted sand off his hands. "I must greet your chieftain. Would you be willing to introduce me?"

So, the old man knew the Friesland custom of having a clan member vouch for a stranger. Heward was sure Haakon wouldn't like it, but better he than Grandmother, he supposed. They rode into the village. People stared as they dismounted, but Boniface seemed unconcerned. It turned out he had a request for Haakon.

"We ask your leave to celebrate the Eucharist tomorrow morning," he said, as the three of them stood by the fire in the great house. "The clan of Haakonii is welcome to come."

Heward watched Haakon brood over the words. He was a broad-shouldered giant of a man, known for his rash temper.

"Why should I allow it?" Haakon snapped. "You say you are not Franks, but you come from their territory. They are Christian and so are you. When they win in battle, they force our people to be baptized, or they kill us. Sometimes they do both."

Boniface nodded. "I have seen it happen across the Frankish lands. I have tried to change King Pepin's mind about it."

Haakon's face darkened at the mention of the name. Heward stared at Boniface. He *knew* King Pepin?

"What I can tell you is that we are here to persuade, not threaten. God sent Jesus to *all* people because he loves us."

Haakon snorted. "I prefer gods with power."

Boniface said, "Ah. I heard that same answer years ago from your great chieftain Dagobert. Yet he gave us leave to celebrate Eucharist."

Haakon's eyes widened. "You knew Dagobert?"

Boniface nodded. "He was a mighty chieftain, who did not fear our persuasion."

Heward smiled inwardly. That might do it. Haakon would love to be compared to the famous Dagobert. Reluctantly, Haakon agreed to let them celebrate the Eucharist.

The next morning, Heward wandered out of the hut still sleepy, blinking at the gray skies. Grandmother, with high color in her cheeks, was unfolding a cloth on a table with Eoban. It was fringed, light blue with white crosses on the edges, beautifully made. Heward recognized it as the first weaving Grandmother did after Mother and Grandfather died. Haakon had offered Grandmother extra money for it, but she had refused to sell. Heward caught sight of Haakon and three elders standing fifty feet off, arms folded across their chests. Haakon's face looked thunderous; he recognized the cloth, too.

Boniface and the others appeared, one of them carrying a great boxy thing. That must be the holy book Grandmother had told him about. They began with a song, bracing and strong, then Eoban read from the book in Latin. Heward knew the sound, though he didn't understand it.

Boniface stood and translated the words. He told how two followers of Jesus healed a crippled man. The healed man walked and leaped for joy. Heward could almost see it in his mind's eye. Then Boniface spoke of Jesus appearing after his death, fixing fish for his followers on a beach, just as Frieslanders did. Jesus asked one man the same question three times: "Do you love me more than these?" Why did Jesus do that? wondered Heward. Was it a charm? But charms were supposed to be pagan.

More singing as bread and wine were set on the table. Heward found himself studying Grandmother. She looked different somehow. Younger? Heward wasn't sure. She stood with hands clasped, her whole attention on the bread and wine. Heward saw how the others watched her with tenderness and pleasure, especially Boniface.

Heward felt something gradually changing around him. Perhaps it was that the wind had died, but now everyone around the altar was silent, focused. Everyone knelt. More words from Boniface, answered by the rest. Boniface lifted the bread above him and held it there. *My body is given for you. Remember me.* Heward didn't know how he knew those words fit this moment, but he did. He looked at Grandmother. She was still, her face calm as pooled water.

Heward had an odd sensation somewhere in the region of his stomach. He was accustomed to thinking of Grandmother as grouchy, difficult, even eccentric. That's what people of the clan thought. That's what *he* thought. His cheeks felt hot with shame. He saw that what had looked like stubbornness in Grandmother was in fact a desperate fidelity. She had lost much, endured much. Now she was receiving the bread as one receiving a treasure, her face lifted like a cup brimming with joy.

All had received the bread now. Boniface stood with his head bowed at the altar, and the silence deepened again. Something was here, thought Heward. It felt strange and strong and new; he was almost dizzy with it. Grandmother and these men seemed to be listening to a voice he could not hear.

Heward felt a twinge of sadness at the loss. He closed his eyes. It came to him then that he was not excluded. A wordless question hung in the air, at once urgent and patient. Would he respond? Heward took a breath, released it. Inside himself, he said, *I'm here. I am listening.*

✦ ✦ ✦

Boniface, Bishop Eoban of Utrecht, and the others named in this story spent the spring of A.D. 754 evangelizing in Friesland. On Pentecost Sunday, they were in the village of Dokkum, preparing to confirm recent converts, when a party of pagan Frieslanders descended on them. Boniface and fifty-three others were killed.

The Unsuitable Princess

Elizabeth of Hungary

Born in 1207 in Bratislava, Elizabeth was the daughter of King Andrew II of Hungary. At the age of four, she was betrothed to Louis, the future landgrave (prince) of Thuringia (a region of Germany), and was sent to the court at Wartburg to be raised with her future husband. She withstood much criticism and unkindness from some courtiers at Marburg Castle, but Louis himself was her best friend. The two fell deeply in love. When Louis was advised to send her back home as an unsuitable wife, he refused, saying that he would rather cast away a mountain of gold than give her up. They married when she was fourteen and Louis was twenty-one.

In 1225, famine struck the country. Elizabeth exhausted her own treasury relieving hunger. She built a hospital near the castle, where she herself attended the poor and sick. She fed nine hundred daily at her gates.

Elizabeth and Louis had two children, Herman and Sophia, and, in 1227, she became pregnant with a third child.

✦   ✦   ✦

"Dear Elizabeth," she heard the sardonic voice say, "one foot in the sewer with the poor, and the other in the convent."

The words were those of Mechtilde, Louis's cousin. Elizabeth could distinguish her clear and clever voice from the group before they rounded the turn in the steep street leading to Marburg Castle.

Yes, she thought, *the barbs are there, and meant to sting.*

"Why ever did your father allow her to become Louis's wife?" said another voice, Birgitta, she thought.

"It has been a farce, from then till now," said Henry heavily. This younger brother of Louis's had stood against her from the first. "I told Louis she was unsuitable six years ago, but he was besotted with her. He is still."

The party came around the curve. Five ladies and four lords on horseback, in fine, bright colors, and three pages with hooded falcons on the wrist.

"O-o-oh," breathed little Georg, the orphan who was helping her. He grabbed their sacks of bread and put them behind her skirts. Georg might be poor, she thought, but he had a crackling good brain in his head. He knew Mechtilde and Henry would be furious at the sight of them taking bread to the gates.

Two overflowing wagon loads of bread had gone down before first light and still there were more beggars.

There is nothing to be done, thought Elizabeth, and she resolved to set a smile on her face. At the sight of them, the party's conversation dropped suddenly to nothing. They halted.

"You are out early, my Lords and Ladies," said Elizabeth.

Lord Philip, the eldest of the party, bowed and said, "As are you, my Princess." His eyes flicked nervously to Mechtilde and Henry.

Mechtilde took in all of Elizabeth from head to toe, her blue eyes slits. Elizabeth wore her usual plain dress and shawl, her dark hair tied back simply. Mechtilde, seven years older, had endeavored always to school Elizabeth in her royal duties.

"I'm out for a breath of air with my friend here," said Elizabeth. "It's such a lovely day, it seems a shame—"

"Shame is the word," hissed Mechtilde. "Our princess parading in the streets dressed like a common serving girl."

Out of the corner of her eye, Elizabeth saw old Gertrude and Emilia toiling slowly up the hill from Mass. At Mechtilde's words, they stopped in their tracks, their eyes alight. They were used to the odd sight of Elizabeth, but to see members of the royal house arguing in the streets! That was a novelty.

"I know, Mechtilde. I am a hopeless case," she said gaily.

Henry burst out suddenly, "I care not how you dress, Princess. I care that you had the bakers up early toiling again. The famine is over. The peasants can find food now. Still you persist in giving food away."

"At the hospice beyond the gate—" began Elizabeth.

"Another of your many charities—" said Henry.

At that, she saw Carl the leather worker stop sweeping and lean on his broom to listen.

Elizabeth tried to smile. "I was only going to say, if you stand on the hospice steps and look around, you'll see many hungry faces."

Henry rode close and leaned his bearded face down to Elizabeth. His voice was suddenly savage. "Someone in this family must look to the safety and security of Thuringia, even if the prince and princess do not. *Rest assured, my Lady. I will have my satisfaction on this.*"

The party heard and swayed as if in a wind. The words were outwardly polite, as they must be. But Elizabeth could not miss what looked like near hatred in his eyes.

Jesu, help him. Help me, she prayed, surprised at her fear.

"My Lord—" said Philip.

"What?" Henry's word burned like acid for an instant in the air.

"May we continue this discussion in a more—private place?"

Henry looked around and saw the peasants watching. "Very well." To Elizabeth he said, "When Louis returns home, he'll hear from me." They rode on.

"Holy Mother," said Georg, staring after them.

Let it rest in God, Elizabeth resolved. Georg hefted his sack; they started down the hill once more.

"By the way, Georg, what about her?"

"What about who?"

"The Holy Mother. Were you addressing her, or did you have a heavenly vision just now?"

Georg looked up, perplexed an instant, then he understood. "My La-dy!" he said exaggeratedly.

She laughed. "Next time, it might as well be prayer, for don't we all, Henry included, need to know the love of God?"

The crowds surged toward the gate. Louis had ordered that the portcullis be closed when she gave out food. Elizabeth chafed at this, but to no avail. Now that she was with child, he feared she would be mobbed.

The secret truth was, she loved to look in their faces. Always she saw pain and sorrow. But when their eyes met, often she also saw a rich bond there. Even with the wretched and despairing, sometimes a simple touch upon the arm would strike a spark of hope between them. Now all she could see were hands thrust through the portcullis grid. Those many hands! Desperate and eager, thin and dirty hands, diseased hands, soldiers' hands with fingers missing, old hands, and down low, little children's hands.

Georg and Elizabeth broke the loaves and handed half to each. And these same hands trembled as they were filled. A lovely ribbon of gladness wrapped itself around Elizabeth's heart again. Jesu must have felt so when he fed the multitudes.

That night, she prayed again for Henry and Mechtilde and the others at court. They were immured against her, she knew. Louis said it was that way with families sometimes. They knew her so well, or thought they did, having known her since she was four. Sometimes knowledge itself was a barrier.

What are the words to break down that wall? Why can I not even explain this joy, let alone share it with them? She held the question in her mind, then felt a question in return.

Did my family understand me?
Ah, she said, *I had forgotten.*

Louis returned two days later. From his bags, he lifted out a lovely rosary of orange coral. He took Elizabeth's hand on his arm, covering it with his own. An embrace would have to wait until they were alone. It was not deemed respectable before the courtiers.

"It's beautiful, Louis. Thank you." She smiled at him, then slowed her steps, seeing distress in his eyes. "Is something wrong?"

"Nothing," Louis answered. "I—only wondered, will Herman and Sophia remember me? A month is a long time to be away."

She laughed and told him how the children asked about him every day. It was only later that afternoon that they had time alone at last. It was a lovely warm day, with bright bands of sunlight to warm the stone floors of the solarium.

"Growing season has started well," said Louis, standing at the window. "Herman and Sophia are bright as two flowers, as are you, my blooming love." He sat down beside her and laid his hand upon her belly. "Your hair is like dark leaves holding the budding life within."

Elizabeth smiled. There was that side of Louis that only she knew—the ardent lover, the poet. Louis held her close, and he remained that way, almost—could it be?—as if he needed comfort. The question came into her mind again.

She said, practically, "There's nothing much to see of the baby. I hardly show yet."

"But I can tell," he said, his voice that warm, contented rumble that she loved to hear. "Will it be a boy or girl?"

"A girl, I think, though your brother and the councilors would prefer another boy."

Louis sighed and sat back. "My brother—always worrying, whether I'm at home or abroad. Will the dynasty be strong? Will the family have abundant heirs? Ah, but not too many! Will the emperor allow us to increase our wealth? Are we as powerful as the other principalities? Are our castles as fine as theirs?"

Elizabeth laughed. "Since you yourself refuse to think of such things, perhaps that's Henry's work here, since he does not sit upon the throne himself."

"His *work* is to worry?" Louis arched an eyebrow. "Your blessed Francis would laugh at that. Surely God has better plans, even for Henry!"

There came a knock at the door. Jutta, Elizabeth's lady-in-waiting and friend, leaned around the door.

"Lord Henry is here to see you, my Lord."

"I will come," said Louis.

"Henry is very angry with me," said Elizabeth. She thought of telling him what had happened on the road, then decided she would not. "What will you tell him?"

Louis stood and smiled. "That you are incorrigibly generous. That we can afford your charity at the gate. That God will bless Thuringia, and our people will love us all the more." He stood, and Elizabeth saw his eyes rest on his bags beside the bench, worry once more in his eyes.

"Louis, what is troubling you?" His cheeks turned pink. That was a surprise; there was no embarrassment between them.

"It is difficult being married to a woman who can read my thoughts," he said. So there *was* something wrong.

"But you know my thoughts, too."

"Later, my love. We will speak later."

Elizabeth sat warming her feet in the sunlight. When she stood up, her foot caught the bottom of his bag. She stumbled, and the bag tipped, the contents spilling out. She gathered up Louis's clothes and felt something heavy in the cloth. She unrolled the cloth, and there lay a Crusader's cross.

Elizabeth's hand began to shake. The emperor had ordered his vassals to the Crusade. This cross was the sign that Louis could not refuse to go. A cry seemed to arch up from Elizabeth's heart, out of her control. Her legs gave way. Jutta came running in, and found her fainted on the floor.

It was the 25th of June, the weather hot. Their party of seventy-five had traveled three days from Wartburg. Louis and his sixty men would join Emperor Frederick in Italy for the voyage to the Holy Land. Two days before they had passed the border of Thuringia, but Elizabeth would not turn back as planned. Louis himself, Lord Philip, even Jutta, her lady-in-waiting, had tried to coax her, but Elizabeth refused.

She rode at Louis's side. What did one more breach of courtly etiquette matter now? She prayed for faith and felt suddenly empty of it. Every moment, she was afraid. Did she look ahead to darkness, to a life all shorn of earthly love?

They came to a river that the party would have to ford.

"Halt," called Louis.

Henry rode to the front. "Enough of this. Order your wife home."

Louis's eyes snapped in anger. "I am the prince, Henry. You are regent only until I return. Remember that." Without a word or a farewell, Henry galloped back.

The two of them rode forward till the horses' hooves were in water. Louis smiled at Elizabeth, but now there was no merriment in his eyes.

"Husband." It was the only word she said. Not even to promise him her fervent prayer could she make herself speak. She began to weep.

"My wife, I know." Louis clasped her hands as if to never let them go. He kissed the backs of both hands, then the palms, then laid his hand upon her belly. "For the safety of our little one, you must go home." He took up a rope and wound it around her wrist. "My friend, my love, my only one," he said, looping the rope around the other wrist. He knotted it to a saddle ring. "God give thee grace."

Jutta came beside her, weeping also. Louis handed Jutta the reins and the rope, and Jutta turned them both away. Behind her, Elizabeth heard the splashing of the horses through the current, the clip-clop as they reached the other side.

"Mercy," she whispered. Jutta came up short and turned the horses quickly to face the departing men.

Elizabeth called to Louis silently. *My love. Farewell.*

Stiff in his saddle, Louis raised one hand into the air, in farewell or in supplication,

Elizabeth could not tell. He did not look back. The party disappeared into the trees.

✦ ✦ ✦

On 11 September 1227, Louis died of the plague at Otranto, Italy. Word of his death reached Elizabeth just after the birth of her second daughter, Gertrude. Upon hearing the news, she ran shrieking through the halls of the castle.

Within weeks, Henry had turned Elizabeth, her children, Jutta, and Isentrude (another lady-in-waiting) out of the castle in the middle of winter. After taking shelter in a barn, they eventually made their way to Kitzingen, where they stayed with Elizabeth's relatives. The relatives soon had plans for her to remarry, something she and Louis had vowed never to do.

Elizabeth found safe places for her children and, in 1228, she took the habit of the third order Franciscan. Sustained as always by her love of God, she built a small house and a hospice for the sick, poor, and aged outside the castle of Marburg. Worn out from the extremities of her work, Elizabeth died on 17 November 1231, not yet twenty-four years old. (All of the above information came from Jutta and Isentrude when they gave evidence for Elizabeth's canonization as a saint.)

Elizabeth's brother-in-law, Henry, seized power, first becoming an ally of Emperor Frederick II, then repudiating him. He became the German antiking, used by Pope Innocent IV in an attempt to oust the Hohenstaufen dynasty from Germany. Henry died at forty-five from the effects of a winter campaign to conquer the neighboring kingdom of Swabia.

The Holy Terror

Catherine of Siena

Catherine, or Caterina as she was actually called, was born in 1347 in Siena, Italy, to Lapa and Giacommo Benincasa. Her father, Giacommo, was a prosperous dyer. Caterina had her first vision of Christ at seven and knew that she wanted to serve God alone. At fifteen, she was given a room at home where she prayed in solitude for three years, leaving it only for Mass. Later, she spoke of having a cell within where she learned who she was in God's eyes, where Christ was her constant companion. At sixteen, Caterina felt that Jesus was asking her to serve in the world, and she joined a Dominican lay order. She fed the hungry and tended the sick during the 1374 plague. Her shining piety soon attracted followers, known as the "Caterinati." She became convinced that the French pope, Gregory XI, had to return the papacy to Rome from Avignon, France. In 1376, she went there to tell him so.

✦ ✦ ✦

From Lady Elys of Turenne in Avignon on 24 June 1376, to Lady Marguerite of Hainault, greetings.

Alas, Marguerite, that you cannot come! I hoped you might brighten my days at Avignon. My dear Pierre left a month since for our chateau in spite of my protestations. (I could not go because little Louis is ill.) English armies are on the move again, and our estates are close to Bordeaux. Fighting could break out at any time. Those vile Englishmen, rooting around Bordeaux like pigs searching for truffles. I hate them!

Louis coughs at night until I am mad with the noise. My maid Sophie sits up with him, of course. A doctor came to bleed him yesterday, and Louis wrestled him like a lion. I told Sophie to stop coddling him. "Hold him down!" I told her. "How else is he to get better? Already he has ruined my plans!"

You would not fear for our safety if you could see the Papal Palace. It sits on a precipice above the River Rhone with enough ramparts and battlements to stop an army of Englishmen. The pope, you know, *bought* Avignon in 1348. It cost a fourth of the papal treasury, but it's worth every centime if it gives our French pope a secure home far from Italy.

The hall where his Holiness, my uncle, holds court is magnificent. Arches leap skyward and bright frescoes cover the walls. (Unfortunately they show God punishing the unfaithful Israelites, not at all a cheerful subject.) The pope's throne is on a dais. His advisers stand behind and whisper in his ear. Princes bring gifts; prelates ask favors and plan policy. Pope Gregory listens for hours on end. My father-in-law, the pope's brother, worries about him. His Holiness is easily taken ill, poor man.

Other business goes on midway down the hall. Courtiers make alliances, buy and sell spices and wool, and plan revenge against enemies. Pierre conducts his business there. At the end is the ladies' "garden of gossip," as I call it. I go there every day. Stories are started, gossip is traded, and delicious schemes are hatched. We may not be Paris, but Avignon *is* cosmopolitan!

Just now we have an entertaining group from Italy. They would hardly be noticed normally, but they are followers of one Caterina Benincasa, a pious Sienese girl said to be a wonder-worker, though she's not even a nun. With her are the lean and lanky Raymond of Capua, a Dominican priest, Giovanni Tantucci, an Augustinian priest, and a high-strung young poet, Neri dei Pagliaresi.

Caterina came to court yesterday for the first time. We were all craning our necks to see her. We assumed she had to be a beauty to draw so many men around her, but we were surprised. She wears a Dominican habit, that of a lay order. Her face is finely molded, but she is small and pale, as if she lately arose from a sickbed. I pushed my way to the front and asked her, through Father Raymond, if she was ill.

She smiled at me, and her whole face lit up a moment. "Yes, but I am greatly refreshed to be here, so close to the Christ on earth. Here it is easy to be in God like a fish in the sea."

What kind of answer is that, I ask you? I will write again.

From Neri dei Pagliaresi in Avignon on 28 June 1376 to Francesco Maltovolti in Siena, greetings.

Caterina and the others have arrived in Avignon! Everyone is well. I waited on the dock four hours, praying all the while, to catch first sight of her ship. It was a sunlit evening with delicious smells in the air, the fragrance of fresh-turned earth, new grass, and flowers.

"There it is!" shouted Father Raymond, for he and Father Giovanni had joined my vigil. Even calm Father Raymond was pink with excitement. Caterina was last down the plank.

I thought again how small she is. A slender wisp, a willow branch bowing in the wind!

She smiled up at me. "Neri! I see you've been worrying again!" And it was true, Francesco. I have been fretting over my old sins again. I am reminded of them here in Avignon, the city Petrarch calls "the Babylon of the West." What a contradiction this place is! The Masses are plentiful. The Divine Office is chanted with pomp, morning, noon, and night. But the people care only about their houses and clothes and the money they can squeeze from the poor. Courtiers vie for power, clerics beg for benefices, archbishops ask permission to raise taxes. Art treasures created to inspire the faithful in church sit on the side tables in cardinals' palaces. Cardinals live openly with their mistresses and children. You can imagine how I see it, I who once sported in the alehouses and wayward streets of Siena. It is too familiar.

Yet this *is* the seat of Christ on earth, as Caterina says. Father Raymond has been preparing the ground for weeks so that Caterina may sow the seed of Christ. He translates her letters to the pope, and he says that his Holiness listens. Pope Gregory seems a man of good intentions, but there are other voices, other influences on him, people who ignore God.

Father Raymond and I spoke of Caterina yesterday, and he agreed that she has the best of both her parents' character in her—all the gentle piety of her father, Giacommo, and all the strength of will of her mother, Lapa. How I wish I had more of that fire, Francesco! I think of the plague, when half of Siena perished. You lost your parents, I my beloved brothers. Caterina lost a brother and five nieces and nephews. People were mad with fear. You remember? We ran away from Siena, while Caterina nursed the sick and dying. Always she trusts in the robust life, *la vita durabile,* our life in God that never ceases. Ah, Francesco, how far I have to go on my journey to God!

Elys of Turenne to Marguerite of Hainault on 12 July.

Thank you for writing so promptly, Marguerite. Pierre hopes to be back soon. The English have withdrawn to the coast.

You say I sound worried over my husband. It is difficult to write of it. I am still beautiful at twenty-nine, but there are younger beauties here, nieces and cousins of cardinals or courtiers. (Some are nieces in name only; they are mistresses of courtiers or priests.) Isabelle of Honnecourt is the widow of Count Denis of Honnecourt, a man of seventy on the day they wed. He died two months since. With her black hair and flashing green eyes, she is unmistakably happier now that he's gone. I see in her face that she is making plans, calculating risks. She plays to win, that one, like a gambler at the tables. *And she watches Pierre*. At present she is away in Paris, so fear is banished for now, though not ended.

You ask about the wonder-worker. Word is that she has two missions. She is to mediate a peace between the pope and those Florentine dogs. She wants him to forgive their latest treachery for the sake of the common people. It is a certainty she will fail. Second, she wants the pope to move to Rome. Unbelievable! As if his Holiness could be persuaded to do such a thing! Rome is partly in ruins. Chaos stands daily at the gates. The powerful families feud with each other or band together to fight other cities. Italians are greasy-haired buffoons, one and all! They will fight unto the day of judgment.

I asked my father-in-law if she is dangerous. He dismissed her. "My dear Elys, the pope has a solid French head on his shoulders about Italy. He knows the court must remain in Avignon."

From Neri dei Pagliaresi to Francesco Maltovolti on 27 July.

I'm sorry to hear of your fall into sin! Remember that God forgives us when we repent of sins. Many times Caterina reminds me of this when I recall my past. I know you grieve that you cannot talk to her, but you have gone to confession. Beg God to stir your soul with courage!

Caterina herself has stirred Avignon. Father Giovanni thinks these people are listening to her teaching, but I fear it is more a matter of outrageous curiosity. The clerics want to trick her into some theological misstep. The courtiers quiz her on Florentine politics, and the women want to prove she's not as pious as she's reputed to be. They laugh when they hear her speak Tuscan, not French or Latin. It hurts me to hear it, but it doesn't matter to Caterina. She cares nothing for the world's opinion. Tomorrow she has an audience with his Holiness. Keep us in your prayer. And remember that Caterina's "gentle Jesus, Jesus love" is in your heart. Be therefore comforted.

From Elys of Turenne to Lady Marguerite of Hainault on 9 August.

Louis is better. I wish I knew what is keeping Pierre. He was due home days ago, but I have heard nothing.

The Sienese wonder keeps working away here. After Communion, she kneels and prays for an hour with arms outstretched. My friends and I sit nearby. Last week Suzanne wondered aloud whether she totes up her food bill while she kneels. Caterina gave no response. Mirielle even pinched her cheek; she was unmoved. But this Caterina does affect people, even those I had thought immune to her. Yesterday, I saw Br. Jean Buffelet from Paris praying and glancing now and then in her direction. He used to be most interested in which brocade to hang in his bedchamber and what wine to serve at table. Now he's praying! And he's not the only one. I admit that even I am drawn by the look on her face in prayer. It's as if she exists in some lovely place, far removed from the world. I do not understand her.

How does the pope himself react? A tight-jawed seriousness settles over his head like a helmet when he hears Caterina's letters. He prays more and listens less to his advisers. He laughs not at all. Even my father-in-law is worried. Caterina appears a naive fool, yet somehow she has power over people. Her attempt to reconcile the Florentines and the pope has come to nothing, as expected, but she continues urging the pope to move to Rome. There is good news, however. The pope agreed to have Caterina questioned by theologians. They will uncover her many flaws. Do you know that she addresses his Holiness as "my little papa" in her letters? And members of her coterie call her "Mama"? She is younger than I!

My father-in-law translated a letter of hers for me. *"Everything rushes on, everything flies away. The more one has loved something in the world, the greater is the pain of losing it."* I thought of all I lost in the plague—my sisters, my young love, Robert. Yes, I know we vowed never to speak of that time again, but I grow afraid, Marguerite. The little Sienese says we must depend solely on God. I believe in God, of course, but what she demands is something altogether different—total dependence on God. The world does not feel as solid and dependable as it once did. My life could change suddenly, as it did in the plague. Write to me soon!

From Neri dei Pagliaresi to Francesco Maltovolti on 15 August.

This city is a viper's nest. The pope's advisers have convinced him to have Caterina examined by theologians. She is not afraid. She believes that the Holy Spirit will give her words and wisdom which no opponent can contradict.

Meanwhile, the French cardinals tell the pope that if he goes, he will be murdered on the road or poisoned once he reaches Rome. What is Caterina's response? I was her copyist for that letter to the pope. "I have prayed to the sweet and good Jesus to take away from you all slavish fear, so that only holy fear may remain. . . . Be of good courage and depart, trust in Christ Jesus; when you do that which is your duty, God will be with you and none can be against you. *Be a man, Father, arise!*"

Pray, Francesco, that Caterina's words will be both a balm and a spur for Pope Gregory.

From Elys of Turenne to Marguerite of Hainault on 20 August.

I can hardly write for surprise. The theologians examined Caterina's teachings and beliefs. She came out *unscathed*. Now the theologians have taken to prayers and fasting! She is a holy terror, that one! Who does she think she is, getting messages from God and ordering the pope to Rome?

Yes, it's true. The pope announced he is going to Rome. That woman is destroying Avignon, and we are powerless to stop her. My father-in-law paces his rooms at night. The pope's elderly father shakes his fist when he sees Caterina. I confess I am filled with rage at her. At Mass yesterday, my fury was building all through Communion, so I decided to test her one final time. I came up behind her as she prayed and drove a long needle into her upturned foot. She never flinched.

Next day—Marguerite! It is as I feared: Pierre is consorting with Isabelle of Honnecourt. Her entourage stopped at our estate after leaving Paris. Pierre carried on with her *at our home.* A friend returned early to Avignon and told me, then she prattled it to the court. Now the ladies stifle their laughter when I enter the room. How I wish you were here! The courtiers here are all liars, sycophants, and schemers, like flowers past their height. They look lovely from a distance, but up close they stink with rottenness—Ah, what have I written? That is how Caterina described the courtiers in one of her letters.

From Neri dei Pagliaresi to Francesco Maltovolti on 2 September.

We have delayed leaving Avignon because Caterina cannot stand on her foot. The doctor says she stepped on a long needle, but she does not recall any such thing.

Her foot may be sore, but her spirit is not. We will depart from Avignon before the pope, leaving him to face those growling dogs, the French cardinals, alone. Yet Caterina is certain his Holiness will do it. She knew through a gift of wisdom that the pope had promised God long ago to return to Rome. He knows the papacy belongs there. She confronted him, and she believes he cannot ignore his vow now. Her efforts on behalf of Florence, sadly, came to nothing, but we can rejoice that Pope Gregory will restore the Chair of Peter to Rome. We come by land. Do not expect us before November, Francesco.

From Elys to Marguerite 1 September.

Pierre strolls in the gardens openly with Isabelle Honnecourt. My father-in-law pats my hand and says, "Be a noble wife, my dear. Bear Pierre many sons. Remember, Isabelle will inherit nothing." Can he not see how my life hangs by a thread? A mere breeze could snap it!

Yes, what you heard is true: Pope Gregory has left Avignon. I watched as the cardinals stood weeping, begging him to stay, warning him he would be murdered on the road.

And old Count Guilliaume de Beaufort, the pope's father, shouted, "You cannot guarantee your safety. I implore you, my son, stay here in Avignon!"

My father-in-law, meanwhile, was white with fury. "You've been duped by Caterina! You are a fool, Roger!"

"You will not speak to me so," the pope said sternly, and all were silent. He said, "God requires this of me. Caterina only reminded me of what I already knew. You would all do well to remember: death is not far off, as it was during the plague. I have steeled myself to death. So must you."

The pope's father threw himself on the ground before his son, sobbing—a pitiful sight! The pope literally stepped over his own father. But I saw his face, Marguerite. He was paying the cost to the last centime, *but he would not be moved.* He rode out of the castle on a donkey. Yes, you read that right. Pope Gregory is riding to Rome on an ass— no doubt it's some reference to Jesus in Jerusalem.

What a calamity for Avignon! Everything lovely and comfortable is gone, the might of kings, the splendor of the Church. I have lost Pierre. My only comfort is little Louis, who sees I am sad and tries to help. What shall I do now? I have no one to turn to. From where shall my help come?

✦ ✦ ✦

Pope Gregory arrived in Rome in December 1376 and began reforms, but he was taken ill and died six months later. Pope Urban VI, an Italian, was elected. Caterina advised him, but Urban proved to be emotionally unbalanced. The cardinals quietly left Rome and elected a rival pope, who went back to Avignon. In 1380, Caterina died, saying she wanted to give her life for the church. It would be seventy years before an uncontested pope would sit on the Chair of Peter in

Rome, but Caterina's strong voice was not forgotten in the debate. For her more than three hundred and fifty letters and her *Dialogue,* she was proclaimed a doctor of the church, one of only three women to be so named.

The One Who Is with Me Is Kind

Teresa of Ávila

Teresa de Cepeda y Ahumada was born in 1515 in Ávila, Spain. Her father, Don Alonso, was an intelligent and devout man. Her mother, Beatriz, had ten children and died when Teresa was thirteen. Teresa had a lively social life and considered marriage, but at twenty she entered Ávila's Carmelite Convent of the Incarnation. For two decades her spiritual life was mediocre. She was often gone from the convent due to illness. Then she found worthy confessors and books on prayer, and she began having mystical experiences. Teresa saw that convent life was not centered on God. A friend suggested that she open a convent with a simpler life, more removed from the world. Teresa did not take it seriously until she prayed, then the will of "his majesty, the Lord Jesus," was clear.

✦ ✦ ✦

My husband and I wait in the porch of the house in Ávila. I heard the bells toll one of the clock a while since. Cicadas scratch their noisy choruses in the August night. Somewhere out of sight a door bangs, a rough voice calls. I jump. Juan snorts, then breaks into a husky laugh.

"Look at us!" he says. "Nervous as two assassins. Only we're plotting with a Carmelite nun, four postulants, and a priest!"

"Hush!" I say. We wait again. It is strange to think where our decisions lead us. I thought at fifteen that I, Juana, average in every way, would never marry, and that my lovely sister, Teresa, Father's favorite, would have her pick of husbands. But Teresa became a Carmelite nun, and here am I, married to Juan and the mother of seven. Now Teresa is secretly opening a new Carmelite convent. Juan and I have lived here for weeks as if the house is ours, while it is renovated as a cloistered convent.

"Why are they not here?" I ask. At that moment, footsteps sound in the cobbled street below. Father Julian rounds the corner. He is a theologian, a good man, if timid and inward-turned. The postulants look excited and apprehensive, like fledglings balancing at the rim of their nest. Teresa comes last. My sister, almost my mama since our mother died, my friend and companion, whom I have envied all my life. Yes? Even now.

"Let us go in," she says, smiling. Juan leads the way through the anteroom, where visitors can speak to a nun behind a curtain, and into the chapel. I start to follow, but stop when I hear Teresa halt. I turn. She is resting a hand on each side of the door frame, her eyes closed. Praying? Perhaps she is simply savoring this moment. She has been a Carmelite nun for twenty-seven years. Tonight she steps out of the noise and busyness of the Incarnation and into the unknown.

She lifts her head and smiles. "There is a passage in Isaiah I love. 'Enlarge the site of your tent. Let the curtains of your habitations be stretched out; do not hold back; lengthen your cords and strengthen your stakes.'"

"What does it mean?" I ask.

"That God wants us always to grow in faith. He takes pleasure in our growing, and so should we."

The chapel smells faintly of whitewash. Planks lie in one corner. We kneel and Father Julian asks God's blessing on Saint Joseph's. The others leave to tour the convent, but I linger.

I say to God, *Teresa may not be afraid, but I am. What will the nuns at the Incarnation do when they find out? What about the*

Carmelite provincial? Will Ávila accept Saint Joseph's? Then the darkest question. *What if the Inquisition is against her?*

The Incarnation Convent has one hundred fifty nuns and is full of visitors and parties. (I lived there as a boarder after Father's death, so I know.) The nuns leave for long visits, for it means fewer mouths to feed. Some girls come because they have besmirched their family's honor, and what can they do but become nuns? Poor things, they aren't meant for religious life. They wear jewelry, put crimps in their veils, and hold parties where young gentlemen gaze soulfully at them through the parlor grille. The Incarnation has many good women, Teresa says, but they strive for holiness in spite of the convent, not because of it.

I hear no answer. I believe my sister has inner promptings from God. But I, Juana, know no such dramatic voices. Have never known them. Does the Lord of all the earth truly take such minute interest in one little Spanish convent of five nuns?

I join the others in the nuns' cells. Each whitewashed room has a stuffed straw bed, blankets, a desk, a chair, and a cross with a candle beneath. They are plain rooms, but spareness, I think, has its own beauty.

Teresa says to the postulants, "In these rooms, your minds and hearts will find rest.

Saint Joseph's will be a quiet place, so that you can hear the still, small voice of God. We will house thirteen nuns, no more, to that same end."

Then she hugs Juan and me. "My dear sister and brother in the heart, thank you for your help! You are the godparents of this new creation."

Then she looks down at me. (My sister is in no way a small woman.) "Juana, don't worry! God set this in motion. He will conquer the details, too."

Juan and I move to an inn and return the next morning, 24 August 1562, for the first Mass. Father Julian brings salmon-colored roses for the altar. They glow in the early morning light. The birds seem thrilled with the coming day, singing to each other in a dizzying round. A covered chalice rests on the altar. After Mass, the Host will be reserved in the tabernacle. At that moment, Teresa says, Saint Joseph's Convent will be born.

Four habits and sets of sandals are folded before the altar. Teresa and I sewed these rough habits, so different from the fine cloth habits at the Incarnation. Teresa pipes an opening song of praise with laughter in it. Juan joins in on Teresa's little drum.

At offertory, the postulants come forward.

"Is it truly your wish to become Discalced Carmelites of the Primitive Rule?" asks Father Julian.

"Yes," they answer, and they are named. Antonia del Espiritu Santo, Maria de la Cruz, Ursula de los Santos, and Maria de San Jose. Teresa gives the first three their habits. Smiling, Father Julian presents the last to his sister, Maria de San Jose.

We all receive the Eucharist. It is months since Juan and I have done so. The church frowns on us receiving often; we are laypeople, after all. In the silence after Communion, even my heart comes to a place of rest. Father Julian takes the chalice to the tabernacle and, with precision, places it inside. He closes the door, turns the key, and kneels before it. His long fingers rest a moment on the door—an intimate, tender gesture. In just that way, I have seen Juan touch the heads of our newborn babies.

"See?" Juan whispers. "Everything has happened without a hitch. You worried for nothing."

But the next morning—disaster!

When I ring the bell at Saint Joseph's, a hesitant voice says, "Who is it, please?"

"Doña Juana de Ovalle." The door opens.

"Thank goodness it's you," says Doña Ursula's voice behind the curtain.

"What has happened?"

"Last night Mother Teresa was summoned back to the Incarnation to answer for her actions."

"Just what I was afraid of! Is she in the convent prison?"

Doña Ursula gives a strange half-laugh. "I asked her that. She said, 'I hope they put me there. At least then I'll be guaranteed some quiet.'" Ursula pauses. "She made me subprioress in her absence. Professed less than a day and here I am."

I reach my hand through the cloth and clasp her hand. "I know it is hard, but be brave. I will pray for you."

She squeezes my hand. "Thank you. Will you go to the Incarnation and tell us what is going on?"

My heart quails at the thought, but I agree. I run back to the inn to find Juan pacing in our room.

"Did you hear?" he says. "The mayor was thundering about Saint Joseph's to a crowd in the plaza. 'Ávila has thirty-six convents and monasteries, and now we must support one more?' The whole town is in an uproar!" He looks at my face, then stops.

I hold on to Juan and cry a little. "My sister is like a knight of Ávila going to battle. I am afraid for her."

We ring the bell at the Incarnation. The door is opened by Doña Matilda. Her face turns sour when she sees us.

"What do you want?"

Juan bows. "We would like to see Doña Teresa, if we may."

"I'll ask Mother Maria, though I marvel you have the impudence to show your faces here, especially you, Doña Juana, who lived under our roof. We know you were involved in this plot." She shuts the door in our faces. When she opens it again, she points grudgingly to the parlor.

I am surprised. Teresa looks exceedingly well, even happy. "What happened?" asks Juan.

Teresa says, "When I arrived, the entire convent was gathered with Father de Salazar, the Carmelite provincial. The nuns spoke first. They said, 'Who does she think she is, starting a new convent without telling anyone?' Mother Maria was furious." Her face darkens; Mother Maria is our cousin. "Some of my friends cried. I felt sad that I am a cause of pain to them."

"What did you do?"

"I knelt before them and spoke of my promptings from God. I showed them my permission from Rome and from the Bishop of Ávila. I said, 'I believe I am following the will of the Lord Jesus in opening Saint Joseph's. I have followed the leading of God as well as I can. If I have done wrong in this, I am sorry.'"

"The provincial ordered the nuns to leave, and asked me many questions." Her eyes begin to dance. "He growled, 'You have made a holy mess for me to clean up.' I agreed that was so. 'Stay here until the uproar dies down, then you may return to Saint Joseph's. If this effort is of God, he will prosper it. You may be a fresh wind in our ancient order. We shall see.'"

I clap my hands. "Then you have his personal permission!"

"Yes," says Teresa, "and I want to dance down the hallway!"

"That is good, especially in light of the mayor," says Juan, and he tells Teresa what has happened.

She says, "Juan, go to Saint Joseph's. Tell them everything. Remind them that if the mayor appears at the door, they are to do what we discussed last night."

Juan rises. "I will go immediately."

Teresa sits back, hands folded in her lap. Even at forty-eight, she has dainty and well-shaped hands. I have our father's hands, broad in the palm with short, round fingers. How I envied Teresa those hands when we were girls!

"What are you thinking?" she asks.

My cheeks grow hot. "How jealous of your pretty hands I once was."

"Bah!" she says. "Comparisons are hateful! Don't waste a moment comparing yourself to me."

"You would not say that if you could look through my eyes."

"Juana," she says, "you have gifts that I have not."

My throat feels tight. I ask, "What gifts are those?"

"You know how to comfort people. You are often a calm center for others. Juan and your children know your gift of listening. The nuns here all remember your kindness."

Envy sits heavily on my shoulder. "I am not brave like you."

Teresa goes to the window and opens the shutters. A shaft of hot sunlight pours into the room. A cart squeaks to a halt in the street below. A boy's voice commands the ox to move. Another shriek of metal, and the cart starts forward.

"I'm not so brave as you think. When I make a decision, I am always timorous. I immediately think I'm doing everything wrong."

I am surprised. "Even about this?"

She sits down. "If I were not certain this is God's will, I would rather stay here than open a hundred convents."

I think of our father, his absolute truthfulness, his holy purposes. How like him Teresa is! He held us to the highest standards without ever raising his voice. (But how I dreaded his disapproving look!) Yet, my sister is not so austere as he. Teresa can be merry, too. She is like a sharp and fragrant spice, one to make you sneeze if you take a great breath of it.

"Juana, do you think God takes notice of you?"

I stiffen. Ever since we were young, Teresa has asked me these odd questions. And she expects answers. I don't know what to say.

At last I shrug. "There is little about me to notice. I love Juan and my children. I obey the church. I try to be happy. That is all."

She shakes her head. "We women have so few choices. To be a woman in Spain today is to feel your wings droop. Someday that will change."

"Not for me," I say, and I see anger in her eyes.

"Why not for you? No one is excluded from God's love. It is love which sets us free."

"I know that is what the church teaches."

Teresa says, "The church teaches this so that you can discover it for yourself. Life in God is an adventure! Any soul, fired with Love, can dare all for Love."

I laugh. "You sound like the knights and ladies in those romances you and Mama used to read behind Father's back!"

That hits the mark. Teresa flushes. She now believes those books were a bad influence on her. Years ago she even wrote one with our brother Roderigo. Now she is silent, her face dark.

"I have offended you," I say.

She sits down. "No. I was only remembering our mother. She was loving and kind but—"

"But what?"

"Mama withdrew too much from living."

"She was often ill," I say defensively.

"I am often ill, yet I live." Teresa's brown eyes are intent. "Juana, you have many strengths, but you will never discover them if you hide as she did."

"Hide?" The word stings me like a wasp bite.

She grasps my hand through the grille. "Mama worried over everything, feared everything. She withdrew from joy, from living. Don't follow her."

I pull back my hand. "How can you say that about our mother?" Teresa is silent. I stand up. "I'm sorry. I must go."

Juan comes back late that night. He delivered Teresa's message and bought food for the nuns. He climbs into bed next to me. This is usually my favorite time. I tell Juan my quiet thoughts, all the things I cannot say in the light. I love to lie with him, comforted by his warmth. Tonight I am stiff and silent, my mind tethered to Teresa's words. I force myself to listen.

"The mayor and the constables banged at the door, shouting imprecations and threats. Do you know what the nuns did? They barricaded the door! The mayor and constables heard, but they could do nothing at all! What brave souls!" I hear pride in his voice, as if they are his own valiant daughters.

He draws me close. "Juana, is something wrong?"

I tell him what Teresa said. "Is she right about Mama?"

"I cannot say, Juana, since I never knew her."

I whisper, "Is she right about me?"

Juan says quietly, "What does your heart tell you, Juana?"

After Juan sleeps, I go out on the balcony. The questions in my head cascade like waterfalls. They are rushing white torrents of questions. Who do I think I am? Why should God want me in the first place? *Does* God take pleasure in my growing? Poor body. Poor self. Is this what it means to grow? It hurts.

It is October now. Little has changed, except that each morning I sit and pray in the garden. I ask for a brave heart. I ask to know God.

The carrots and beans have been harvested. Ripe apples almost drop into my hand. The last sheltered roses flame into bloom. I am envious of growing things. They do not have to obey God as I do. Or perhaps that is wrong. Perhaps they have nothing, *are* nothing, except obedience to Creation. As for me? Still I hear no vivid voices. Yet, sometimes I feel I am not alone in the garden, and the one who is with me is kind.

I travel to Ávila, alone this time. Teresa is still at the Incarnation. The mayor's lawsuit is not yet resolved, but many Ávilans now support Saint Joseph's. We go to Sunday Mass at the cathedral. The priest is Felipe Sega, the new papal nuncio. A large, overbearing man, he thunders a passage from Saint James.

"God opposes the proud, but gives grace to the humble. Cleanse your hands, you sinners. Purify your hearts, you double-minded. Lament and mourn and weep!" He pauses dramatically. "Yet there are in Ávila some who do not obey God." A sudden hush; even the babies are still. "Their leader is a *woman,* a restless, disobedient, and contumacious gadabout—"

God help us! He's talking about Teresa. I feel a flush of embarrassment travel from my toes to my hairline.

Father puts his head down like a bull preparing to charge. "Under the cloak of piety, she has invented false doctrines and left the enclosure of her convent against the orders of her superiors." He looks straight at us. I am riveted to my seat in agony. "And she teaches as if she were a professor! This is contrary to Saint Paul, who said that women are not to teach!"

I venture a look at Teresa. She has a hand over her mouth. Is she as stung by this rebuke as I? Our eyes meet and, like a shock of cold water on my hot cheeks, I realize that Teresa is hiding a laugh. My heart slows its pounding. Something new is here. In this crowded church, with that condemning, wrought-up priest, I am strangely relieved. My turbulent questions flow into a pool of still water. I feel again the kindness in the garden.

✦ ✦ ✦

Teresa returned to Saint Joseph's three months later. In 1567 the Carmelite general asked her to open more convents. Traveling through rough country, bargaining with mule drivers, staying at filthy inns, Teresa founded convents in ten cities. She died in 1582 at Alba de Tormes, one of her foundations.

Teresa wrote *The Interior Castle, The Way of Perfection, A Life,* and other books. Often she wrote only one draft because she had no time for revision. "I only wish I had two hands to write with," she once said, "so as not to forget one thing while I am saying the other." Teresa was declared a doctor of the church in 1970 for her theological eminence, the authority of her writings, and the holiness of her life.

God Alone

Francis Xavier

Francis Xavier was born in 1506 of a noble Spanish family. He studied theology and philosophy at the University of Paris and became close friends with Peter Favre and Ignatius of Loyola. Ignatius led Francis—or Francisco, as he was known—through Ignatius's newly completed Spiritual Exercises. With four others, the Company of Seven became priests and formed the Society of Jesus (Jesuits).

In 1541, at the pope's request, Francisco set sail for Portuguese India to serve new converts there. The voyage took eighteen months, and many people on the journey died from fever. Francisco helped the sick onboard and in the hospital at Goa, India. He traversed the southern coasts of India and ministered to the low-caste Paravas, fishermen, and pearl divers who were oppressed by both Muslims and Hindus.

✦ ✦ ✦

Francisco stretched out for a few hours of sleep. They would leave Manappad at dawn for Cape Comorin. The wind creaked the timbers and lifted the palm leaves that formed the walls and roof of his hut. It was, he decided, like being onboard ship, lying still while all around was incessant movement.

A runner had come with the news that Badaga horsemen had attacked the Paravas of Cape Comorin because the villagers were Christian and therefore allied to the Portuguese in this civil war. Many villagers had been killed. Those who escaped ran for their catamarans and reached the offshore rocks. Francisco pictured them now, huddled on the barren rocks off the bottom tip of India. They were alive but trapped, with the boiling sun beating down and the raging wind battering them.

Francisco held up the Paravas to God, like Moses with his hands raised over the Red Sea. He reminded God of their suffering. He begged for relief and help. *You love and help us also, my Lady. Pray to the Father for these lambs. . . .*

A voice. He opened his eyes. Still dark.

Antonio stood in the doorway. "It is time, Great Father." Francisco had grown to depend on this Parava boy. Antonio was his translator, guide, and cook. He said little, but he was bright, having learned Portuguese in the market in Goa.

Francisco took his breviary, frayed biretta, and writing materials and followed Antonio to the beach. A bonfire billowed in the high wind, sending up sparks. Clothes stood out from people's bodies like little flags. Breakers thundered ashore.

Twenty catamarans were piled high with food, water, and cloth to make shelters. Each catamaran had a crew of four. When Francisco had announced his intention to help the Cape Comorin Paravas, the local Portuguese traders and these poor villagers had gathered food, water, and cloth to help. The catamarans would follow the coastline of India south to Cape Comorin.

Francisco felt a tug on his cassock. It was little Anna.

"Who will ring the bell and teach us songs while you are gone?" she asked. Francisco picked her up, kissing her cheek.

"My bell is in my hut," he said, and Antonio translated. "You may keep it until I return. But remember, you may ring it only to call the children to sing the songs of God." Anna smiled, satisfied.

"Let us pray to God, our Father," he shouted over the wind. "God in heaven, give us your saving help. Be with us as we journey. Keep us safe. Help us to reach our brothers and sisters and protect them from further attacks, in the name of Christ. Amen." Even to Francisco, the prayer seemed tiny against the pounding surf and the massive wind.

Old Paulo and his son, Juan, a broad and silent fellow, would pilot Francisco's catamaran. They motioned to Francisco and Antonio. They pushed into the breakers and rode up one foaming wall of water, down again, and up the next, all of them paddling fiercely. Another three waves and Paulo raised his paddle in triumph. They had crossed the breakers.

Francisco looked back. Eighteen of the twenty boats were out. He watched, relieved, as the last two made it. All his people safe for now. He studied the shore, then concentrated on paddling. After a good while, he looked back. They had hardly moved. He still could see the southern edge of Manappad. Paulo shouted over his shoulder in Tamil.

"Paulo says the winds are against us. It will be a hard journey," said Antonio. Francisco put his whole body into rowing. Forward, in, down, pull. Again. Again. He allowed nothing to break his concentration. By midday, the sun on the water was blinding, the heat ferocious. The empty spots where the rowers knelt were tight for the Paravas, who were small, compact people. For Francisco, who stood more than six feet tall, they were cramped in the extreme. The bags of rice around him were immovable as pillars. His leg was asleep. He rose, gripping the rice bales; the leg gave way and he swayed dangerously.

"Father!" cried Antonio in alarm.

"I'm all right," Francisco said, and found a different position. The hot wind boiled around him. He was thirsty again, and his body ached. But he who had completed the Spiritual Exercises of Ignatius knew how to discipline his mind. He pictured Jesus as a boy, not much younger than Antonio, teaching in the Temple at Jerusalem. Francisco tried to hear what young Jesus was saying. He visualized the back-and-forth conversation, the questions, proposals, Jesus quoting the Holy Scriptures.

It was six days later. The rowers' muscles were cramped from kneeling and paddling. No one spoke now. Francisco could no longer picture Gospel stories. He simply hung on God like the baby monkey he'd seen in Africa, clinging to its mother high above the ground in a tree. That evening, Francisco called the boats to shore. The men squatted in a semicircle on the sand.

"How far have we to go?" he asked. Paulo hesitated. Francisco could see the old man did not want to disappoint him.

"We are less than half way there," translated Antonio.

Francisco looked around. Seventy-nine hollow-eyed men. Their skin was blistered from the sun, their hair caked with salt. They looked skeletal; some were shivering with fever.

"We return to Manappad, brothers," Francisco said.

A sigh went up from the men. A sigh of relief, and of sorrow. With the wind at their backs, they were back in Manappad the next day.

The next evenings, Francisco sat on the beach, writing. He had the same habit in Goa, Cochin, Tuticorin—anywhere that ships and boats came in and gulls called and he could watch the ocean. In busy ports, the bustle and noise made for him a paradoxical place of rest. Perhaps, he thought, it was because no one could own the ocean.

He was writing to Father Mansilhas, his fellow Jesuit in Tuticorin, warning of the Badaga attacks. "It is the worst pain in the world to see the great troubles of these unfortunate Christians. Worst of all is one Cosme de Paiva, a despicable Portuguese captain. He is behind this war. He sells horses to the Badagas, and because of the money he makes, he refuses to stop selling. The actions of Portuguese like him are a permanent bruise on my soul."

Then he began a letter to Ignatius. He was far from Rome, but when he was dispirited, he needed to reach his friends, even if only with words. He was describing the situation of the Paravas when a hand touched his shoulder.

It was Paulo and his wife, Maria, the village matriarch. She was a small woman and, like her husband, had few teeth left, but intelligence shone in her eyes. The high status of Parava women was a rarity among Indians. It was one more thing separating the Paravas from other peoples, for this custom ran counter to Hindu and Muslim beliefs about women.

Paulo and Maria squatted on the sand. After a time, Maria made a broad sweep of her arm as if to show the shore, the sky, the beach, and the mountains.

"God alone," she said.

Paulo nodded. "Because of his love."

Francisco forced himself to lift his head and look. The catamarans were beached; their high, winglike nets swayed in the wind. The sun shown just above the Ghat Mountains in the west. Glowing pink clouds scudded across the eastern sky. It was splendid, a tropical evening lovely enough to make your heart ache. For a moment, Francisco put down his pen. He consciously allowed himself to take it in. He began to relax.

For many months, he had been battling on in his work, his head down, concentrating, praying, ministering to the Paravas. Was he missing something? Paulo and Maria seemed at peace, happy to simply sit and look. He must pray about it.

His mind strayed back to the Cape Comorin Paravas. Could the flotilla try again? He didn't know the Tamil word for wind, but his apostolate with these people was chiefly one of smile and gesture. Speech rarely served his needs.

"Wind," he said in Portuguese, and made the sound of wind. Paulo and Maria nodded. Then he pantomimed a slower, gentler wind. "Tomorrow?" he asked in Tamil.

Paulo and Maria shook their heads. No, the wind would not drop tomorrow. Maria pointed south and west behind them. There, just visible in the distance, was a patch of sky blurred red. She and Paulo pantomimed wind. Francisco shrugged his shoulders, lifted his eyebrows, not understanding.

Paulo pretended to shield his eyes, then rubbed them furiously. The meaning dawned on Francisco. A dust storm was coming, propelled by the postmonsoon wind. He stood up. The sooner he and Antonio started their fifty-mile trek to Cape Comorin, the better. They would carry no supplies; he would have to beg help from the local Portuguese on the coast. He didn't know how to accomplish it all, but he set that fact aside. God would provide, if he did his part.

Francisco, Antonio, and Juan leaned into a shrieking red miasma that drove dust into their eyes and filled their mouths with grit. They could see barely five feet in front of them. Juan led the way. Maria had insisted her son come along.

"Keep alive the Great Father," she had ordered. (Antonio had translated the words with a grim smile.)

Juan and Antonio had knives and staffs to fend off tigers and jackals. Juan told them to watch for snakes and scorpions, and proved his warning a mile out of Manappad. With the tip of his dagger, he launched a deadly scorpion into the air and off the trail.

They made seven miles the first day, only eight the next, the dust pushing them back at every step. That night they found an empty palm-leaf hut. Francisco went down to the beach to pray. He was so spent he could barely hold himself upright against the wind. He managed only one word of prayer, *help,* repeated over and over. At twilight, Juan came and stood three feet away, his back to Francisco, his dagger in his hand.

Francisco said, "Juan, I am fine. Go to bed!"

Juan shook his head. "Badagas," was all he said.

In the darkness, Francisco at last lay down in the hut and fell asleep instantly. He woke again, disoriented, thinking he was back at the College of Sainte Barbe in Paris and his bed had grown unaccountably hard. Then he remembered—a sound. Footsteps. A tiger? He sat up. Then, clearly, he heard a horse blow out a gusty breath. *Badagas.* No other natives had horses.

At the door Antonio stood, pointing up. Into the trees? Antonio nodded. Francisco turned back to wake Juan, but Antonio stopped him. Up, he motioned again. Just then Juan sat up fully awake, without a sound. Francisco climbed. Within seconds, Juan and Antonio were in the next tree. Less than a minute later, nine Badagas rode into the clearing.

If the Badagas looked up, they would easily see the three men in the trees. But the horses had already trampled their footprints. The men lit a fire in the lee of the hut, taking their ease. What if they were still there in the morning?

Straddling a branch, his arm looped around the trunk, Francisco commended himself to God. He prayed for the safety of Juan and Antonio, and for the Paravas. As the Badagas below ate their food, he prayed for them. They also belonged to God, the God of mercy who sent down rain on the just and the unjust, the God who cast light into the depths of each living soul, revealing everywhere and to each one his love.

As the dusty sky turned red with dawn, the Badagas rode off. Francisco, Antonio, and Juan resumed their journey, foraging for coconuts and mangoes and drinking from a stream for water. That afternoon, an amazing, nearly miraculous thing happened. The dust storm ended. The vivid world was restored to their sight. Blue sky brightened above. The ocean was vibrant blue-green, the wind was gentle and cooler. Francisco felt the balm from God.

Two days later, they watched a lone catamaran sail toward them. The rocks in the distance were a bright reflection. Francisco opened the bag at his side, filled with medicinal potions. Antonio had begged some rice— it was pitifully small, but it was a start. Juan had jugs of water and some cloth. As always when the wind died, mosquitoes fed on their bare arms and flies buzzed in their faces. The catamaran slid onto the sand. A man and two boys climbed out, their legs unsteady.

"Great Father," croaked the oarsman.

"Juan, water," said Francisco. Juan poured water into a bowl.

"Thank you, thank you." They bowed and drank, lifting the bowl high, pouring the water into their mouths without touching their lips to the rim, a Parava custom.

The man said, "We knew you would come, Great Father."

"I remember. You are Andres," said Francisco.

Andres smiled. "Yes. These are my sons, Bartolomeo and Filipo."

"Thank you for saving us," said Filipo.

"The mercy is from God to you," said Francisco. "We come with food, water, shelter, and news. The Badagas are gone up the eastern coast, far from here."

At that, Andres sat down suddenly in the sand. His face twisted; he began to cry. Francisco squatted beside Andres and touched the man's shoulder. The boys, too, leaned close for comfort. *What these people have endured,* Francisco thought, and then, *It is now when I see God, now when I know precisely what I must do.*

Soon all the Paravas were on shore. Thirty-five from Cape Comorin were killed or missing. Nine had died on the rocks, including three babies. They would bury the dead tomorrow. They served food and water and staked the cloth for shade. Francisco went from person to person, blessing them and giving medicines. The healthier men began gathering palm leaves to rebuild the burned huts. That evening, Francisco baptized the one newborn baby who had survived. And he taught the children songs.

Francisco carried his writing materials to the shade of a palm tree on the beach at Cape Comorin. It was three weeks later, and he was still writing his letter to Ignatius. He explained why more Jesuit priests were needed in India. Ignatius knew this, of course, but it never hurt to remind him.

Francisco studied the breakers, thinking, *From here, where am I to go? Back to busy Goa?* He held still in his spirit. Then, as in Manappad, he consciously relaxed. A feeling came to him, a feeling that had been hiding inside him these last few weeks in Cape Comorin. Some new place, not yet visible, was beckoning, and he was longing for it the way he longed on his voyage to India for the first sight of land, leaning out over the prow of the ship on fine days. A voyage might help his sometime feeling of emptiness. Or perhaps the emptiness must be borne, like Saint Paul's thorn in the flesh. He wished he could ask Ignatius and Peter about it.

For a moment he allowed himself to remember their youthful days in Paris—their conversation, their camaraderie, the sudden shining insights, the bursts of laughter, their joined prayer. How he hungered to see them! The last letter from Ignatius had hinted he might order Francisco home. But he did not want to leave! There was too much to do! If he went to Rome, he would be gone for three years from India and the East—and yet, to see his friends and comrades once again.

. . .

Suddenly energized, he wrote, "I beg you not to forget me. I live in such need of your help. For my great comfort, and to keep you always present, I have cut out the signatures from your letters, written out in your own writing, and I carry them always with me." He touched his heart and heard the crinkle of parchment; the names were pinned inside his cassock.

Antonio came up behind him.

"Great Father," he said, "A runner is here with news. The Badagas have attacked Tuticorin."

✦ ✦ ✦

When the civil war ended two years later, Francisco was depressed and weary with overwork. He took a voyage to the islands of the Moluccas, and there had a brief month of rest and retreat. He met an educated Japanese traveler, Anjiro, who became a convert and his guide during the two years they spent in Japan. Francisco toured his missions in India once more and departed in 1552 for China, then closed to foreigners. But this goal he would not attain. He died of fever on the island of Sancian off the coast of China. He was canonized in 1662 and is the patron saint of missionaries.

The Gentle Mother

Elizabeth Ann Seton

Elizabeth Ann Bayley was born in 1774 in New York City. Her father was a noted physician. Elizabeth's mother died when she was three. Dr. Bayley remarried, and Elizabeth and her sister were farmed out to relatives. They rarely saw their traveling father. But when she grew up, Elizabeth and her father became close. At twenty, she married William Seton, son of a prominent family. They had five children. Elizabeth was a devoted member of Trinity Episcopal Church.

When William's father died, he assumed responsibility for the struggling family business and eight younger siblings. Soon he showed signs of tuberculosis. As his TB worsened, William, Elizabeth, and their daughter Anna Maria sailed to Italy to see the Filicchis, for whom William had worked. He died there on 27 December 1803. Elizabeth and Anna Maria stayed with the Filicchis for three months due to bad weather. It was there that Elizabeth became interested in the Catholic church.

Elizabeth's conversion, however, was not the individual matter it would be today. Wars had been fought over whether nations would be Protestant or Catholic. Oppression of minority religious groups was common. People of conscience on both sides were imprisoned, tortured, and killed. It was into this divisive situation that Elizabeth stepped when she returned to New York.

✦   ✦   ✦

The Seton family had customary seats in the twenty-third pew on the right side of New York's Trinity Church. But today, and for four weeks past, Elizabeth Seton sat in a side pew, facing east. She looked on the bare altar from the side. The Reverend John Henry Hobart stood in profile to her, finishing his sermon.

"Our Lord Christ says, 'When you pray, go into your room and shut the door and pray to your Father in secret, and your Father who sees in secret will reward you.' And so, my friends, we are to pray in the secret places of our hearts to the God who orders and understands all. We are to follow God where he leads, in obedience, trusting him to find the way."

The music of the closing hymn swelled. *Is this my secret place?* Elizabeth wondered. She was sitting here because, from this spot, she was facing the altar of Saint Peter's Catholic Church one block away. Her body was here, but in secret, her spirit was there, with the Irish and German immigrants who were receiving the Blessed Sacrament. What would the Reverend Mr. Hobart say if he knew of her continuing longing for the Catholic faith? What would her family say? She tried to focus on God, but guilt and fear assailed her.

When she was a little girl, she had known the silent presence of God in the fields and on the beach, where she sat on a rock singing hymns to the sea. Separated from her mother by death, and from her father by his work in Albany, she had been comforted in her loneliness. But she felt no comfort now.

She looked around. The church was nearly empty. Mr. Hobart stood talking to the last congregants. Coming toward her was Mrs. John George, a noted matron in New York society. She was twenty years older than Elizabeth, tall, and dressed in silks, her curls carefully in place.

"My dear Mrs. Seton," she said.

"Mrs. George," said Elizabeth.

"I wanted to express my sorrow for your recent sad loss."

Elizabeth's throat was suddenly tight. William. The final touch of his cold hand. Her kiss on his forehead. Her husband was gone, flown. It had been a gray, cold day when they laid his tortured body to rest in far-off Italy.

"Thank you," Elizabeth managed to say.

Mrs. George patted her hand. "And it is a pleasure, indeed a relief, to see you back at Trinity Church these past Sundays. We all understand, you know. Faced with such a loss, is it any wonder your faith was momentarily swayed by foreign influences?"

So, the story of her interest in the Catholic church was making the rounds.

Elizabeth said carefully, "You have traveled much in Italy, I believe. Do you know the Filicchi family? They are prosperous merchants of Pisa with many connections in New York."

"Yes, I have heard of them."

Elizabeth's fingers tightened on her purse. She pictured Filippo Filicchi carrying her husband down a flight of steps to the carriage for a ride only four days before William died. Antonio Filicchi had sailed with her and Anna Maria back to New York to protect them from the drunken ship's captain.

She said, "I wonder if the stories you have heard bear any relation to the truth? My husband worked for the Filicchis. They were a great comfort to us in my husband's last days. They were and are still our faithful friends." Her voice was shaking.

Mrs. George sniffed. "I'm sure they are faithful. They even sound cultured. But here in America, the Catholic presence is a different matter. Our Catholic immigrants are wretched and unsightly, little more than a public nuisance."

Elizabeth had only yesterday taken food to an old German man who had paradoxically comforted her with his kindness. She stood and said stiffly, "Thank you for the condolences, Mrs. George. I must be going."

"Of course, Mrs. Seton. No doubt your children have taken their father's death hard. I shall pray for them, and for you."

"And I," said Elizabeth, "shall pray for you, Mrs. George."

A thunderstorm was threatening. Elizabeth could hear it rumbling in the distance. The windows were open, but the air was hot and still this afternoon. She was trying, despite a staggering headache, to write a letter to her friend Julia Scott. She had to put the best face on things so Julia wouldn't worry.

"The occupation of mending and turning odd things to the best account and teaching the little ones and having them always at my elbow, you'd believe it is easier to pray than to write. I clean my own room, wash the small clothes, and have more employment in my present situation than ever."

The headache grew worse. She should eat, but food had no appeal. She lay down on her bed. The funeral for Rebecca Seton, William's sister and her closest friend, had been four days ago. In the old, easy days, she and Rebecca had read evening hymns together. They had followed the service of holy days at Trinity and shared the kiss of peace. Now Rebecca was gone, like all the others. First William's father, then her own Papa, then William, and now Rebecca. She had held them all in her arms as they died. *They have all gone above the blue horizon. And I am left behind.*

A sob escaped her. She whispered, "Everywhere I turn, O Lord, I find death, misery, and loss. I feel no comfort, no solace. My soul is paralyzed. You were a pillar of cloud by day for the Israelites, and a sentinel of fire at night. Can you not lead me in the same way?" There was a hesitant knock on the door. Elizabeth swallowed and called out, "I'm all right, dears! Give me another few minutes to rest."

"Yes, Mother," answered a voice from the other side.

"Our Father, who art in heaven," she murmured, "hallowed be thy name. Thy kingdom come—" The headache was a massive boulder of pain. She tried to edge around it, peer beyond it. She focused on each individual word of prayer. "—the kingdom, the power, and the glory, forever and ever. Amen."

She opened the book Mr. Hobart had given her, *Dissertation on the Prophecies,* by Thomas Newton. "The pope is advanced by some commentators to be the Antichrist within the church. . . . Many good men lament the prevalence of popery and wickedness in the world." Newton wrote that Catholics would be punished in hell. But then, Antonio's wife, Amabilia, had written last week. She said Catholics were taught that all Protestants were condemned to hell. Elizabeth's head, her heart, her chest hurt.

She put down the Newton book and with her other hand picked up *Introduction to the Devout Life,* by Saint Francis de Sales. The biography at the beginning comforted her. Here was a solidly holy man who treated Protestant and Catholic alike with kindness, seeing always the individual first, the religious beliefs after. Could she at least be guided by his attitudes, his life?

This decision was agony. No matter what she decided, she would anger, hurt, and disappoint dear friends or dear family. Worse, she sometimes feared that, in the process of deciding, she was becoming neither Protestant nor Catholic, standing apart from the entire Body of Christ. Tears ran past her temples into her hair.

There was a second knock on the door.

"Yes?" she said. The door opened a crack.

"Mother?" It was Anna Maria. "May we come in?"

Hastily, Elizabeth wiped her tears. Her five children came into the room, Anna Maria, the oldest at eight, held baby Rebecca on her hip. They had heard her crying; they all looked stricken.

"Poor Mama!" said Kit, William Jr., and Richard. They patted her shoulder, her feet, anywhere they could touch. They didn't understand the complexities, but they were such tender creatures!

A knock came on the outer door. Anna Maria ran to open it.

"Signor Filicchi!" Elizabeth heard her shout in delight. "Come quickly to Mother."

Elizabeth forced herself to stand. It would not be proper to greet him lying in bed. Antonio Filicchi, tall and striking, kissed each child and made the sign of the cross on each head.

"How is the little American family today?" he asked. And then, looking into Elizabeth's face, he paused.

"I see the gentle mother is feeling sad."

"It is—a difficult day," Elizabeth admitted.

"You grieve for your dear friend." Antonio's long face was serious. He put a hand on her shoulder. "Yet God is helping you at every moment."

Elizabeth nearly gave way at his sympathy. Antonio was a strong rampart to steady her when she was tottering.

"And you are in turmoil about the Catholic church," he said.

"Yes," said Elizabeth. A laugh broke from her, half bitter, half hearty. "I have been weighing, judging, questioning, and worrying. And then I say to God, 'What puny human beings we are! I am an atom. You are God.'"

Elizabeth had tea ready in the sitting room. The Reverend Mr. Hobart would arrive soon. Last year at this time, she would have served cake. But those days were gone. She could not afford a maid or a cook now. She stopped in front of a mirror, smoothed her hair, and straightened her dress. A knock came. She opened the door.

She smiled and said, "How good to see you, Mr. Hobart. Please come in." John Henry Hobart stepped carefully into the room.

"Mrs. Seton," he answered. His voice was deep and sonorous. He knew how to use it to good effect from the pulpit. His clothes as always were neat and well cut. His red hair curled in the heat, and his bald head was bright with sweat. John Henry Hobart was not a handsome man, but Elizabeth had long thought that his physical drawbacks only served to make him more notable spiritually. He sat down across from her.

"Would you take tea?" she asked.

"Please," he said, and took several sips in silence.

"The afternoons are hot," Elizabeth said to start the conversation.

"Indeed," he answered, his voice tense. He took out her most recent letter to him and said, "Mrs. Seton, do you remember the first time we spoke of the Roman Catholic church?"

"Yes. It was the Sunday after Anna Maria and I arrived home. You told me I was influenced by sorrow for my poor William. You said my infatuation with things Catholic would burn off like a fog on a hot summer's day once I was back at Trinity Church."

Mr. Hobart said, "That, to my great distress, has not happened. Our simple, affecting worship at Trinity seems not to have cleared your mind, as I'd hoped."

"That is why I wrote to you," said Elizabeth. "I am weighing things, you see. I want to ascertain the Episcopal teachings on some important questions. What does the Episcopal church teach about the real presence of Christ in Holy Communion? Is the Lady Mary truly the Mother of God? I long to know these things, Mr. Hobart! It would help me to decide."

Mr. Hobart said, "Truly, Mrs. Seton, I wish to be of help to you, but I am frankly—appalled. You focus on these questions and ignore the rest."

Elizabeth stiffened, but she said in a calm voice, "What have I ignored?"

Mr. Hobart said emphatically, "Your Huguenot ancestors suffered for their faith at the hands of this same Catholic church. How can you turn your back on your own forebears?" His face reddened. "Madam, you were born a Protestant. You must remain one!"

Elizabeth looked at him in dismay.

At the sight of her face, he said, "Forgive me. I should not—give me a moment." He stood and walked to the window. He said, "Have you read any of the books I gave you?"

She said evenly, "I have read all of them, Mr. Hobart. How could I not? These past four years, you have been my spiritual guide. You have encouraged me, given me many books to read. You remind me always to be mindful of the heavenly joys—" Her throat tightened. She stopped.

Mr. Hobart came back to his seat and gestured toward the side table. "Yet I see you also have books from your Catholic friends."

Elizabeth picked up the book. "These are the writings of a good and holy man, Saint Francis de Sales. I wish you might read them."

"Not at present, thank you," he said.

Elizabeth watched him, puzzled, then she understood. "You do not approve of me reading Catholic books."

"No, I do not."

"Yet you encourage me to read your books. Is it not fair to examine the arguments of both sides?"

"I do not believe their books will truly benefit you."

Elizabeth said, "So you mistrust the Filicchis, even though they have shown themselves to be people of deep faith."

"Their faith may be deep," said Mr. Hobart, "but I believe it is wholly mistaken." Emotion played over his face. "I had thought this storm had passed, since you have attended either Trinity Church or Saint Paul's for the last six weeks."

Shocked, Elizabeth stared at him.

Mr. Hobart said, "Yes, your friends and I have been keeping an eye on you."

"A true friend," said Elizabeth quietly, "would not lower himself to spying."

Mr. Hobart's face went red. Then he said, "What do your Italian friends say about your attending Trinity Church?"

It was Elizabeth's turn to turn red. All her previous visits from Antonio and her letters from Amabilia and Filippo had been supportive, telling her to pray and to trust that God would give her light for her dark path.

But Filippo's last letter had scored her soul. "You act," he wrote, "as if you think that God is not to be obeyed without the consent and advice of your friends."

"They are—upset with me," she admitted.

"Is that what a true friend would do?"

Elizabeth said sharply, "You are also upset with me."

In a voice of genuine distress, Mr. Hobart said, "I must say, Mrs. Seton, this conversion business of yours is—the most annoying— unwarranted, perplexing affair I have faced as a pastor. I seem powerless to lead you back to the right path!"

Elizabeth saw suddenly how vulnerable he was. Her questions had shaken him to the core. He was her shepherd, and in his eyes, she was a lamb straying close to a chasm.

She said, "Am I not to follow where God leads?"

"I do not believe God is leading you there," said Mr. Hobart. He paused for thought, then said slowly, "People say that you are deluded by your grief over Mr. Seton. Some even call you a fanatic."

Elizabeth said wearily, "I know the tales being told about me. The kinder ones say I am mad. I am a plain scandal to the rest."

He said pleadingly, "My dear Mrs. Seton, you must understand. If you become Catholic, your family, the Bayleys and Setons both, will turn their back on you. They will give no financial help for you or the children, for that would be supporting this delusion."

"My sisters-in-law, Cecilia and Harriet Seton, support me."

"They are mere girls," said Mr. Hobart. "Their parents will soon stop them."

Elizabeth stood and walked to the window. Carriages rolled past. People went about their business. She had been lonely as a girl. She would be far lonelier now.

She said dully, "Yes, I know what will happen, but I cannot ignore God's will."

Mr. Hobart said quickly, "But how can you be sure this *is* God's will? What if these Italians are influencing you? They may be well-intentioned, but they are luring you away from the truth, away from true, primitive Christianity and into their corrupt and false church."

She turned to face him. In a shaking voice, she said, "When I have been at Mass, I have felt the presence of God, the same God you so eloquently describe in your sermons."

Mr. Hobart stiffened; she saw she had offended him. The ache inside her became physical. Her old and honored bond with Mr. Hobart was evaporating before her eyes.

"My home of plenty and comfort is gone. The affection of friends, my husband, my sister, lost." She caught up the last word, then stilled herself. "I am following God as best I can, Mr. Hobart, and God is pulling my heart to Rome."

✦ ✦ ✦

Eight months later, Elizabeth told the priest at Saint Peter's Church that she wished to become Catholic. In 1808, after three years of being ostracized in New York, Elizabeth moved her family to Baltimore, Maryland, a state where Catholicism was more accepted. With the help of the archbishop of Baltimore, John Carroll, Elizabeth made plans to open a school for poor children. Young women joined her, and the Sisters of Charity of Saint Joseph, the first religious community in the United States, came into being. They moved to the mountain town of Emmitsburg and opened the nation's first parochial school. Elizabeth Seton, now Mother Seton, kept her children with her as the new community grew.

After the deaths of her two sisters-in-law, Cecilia and Harriet Seton, Elizabeth's oldest daughter, Anna Maria, died of TB. Then Rebecca died from the effects of a fall.

In later years, Elizabeth Seton was reconciled with nearly all her relatives and friends in New York. The Reverend John Henry

Hobart, later an Episcopal bishop, spoke of her unmistakable holiness. Mother Seton died of tuberculosis on 4 January 1821, surrounded by a solid community of fifty sisters. She is the first American-born saint to be canonized.

Sacred Fire

Frédéric Ozanam

Born in 1813, Frédéric Ozanam grew up in Lyon, France. His father, Jean Antoine, a physician, was a man of splendid character. His mother, Marie, was intelligent and well-read. Both were devout people, well loved in Lyon's slums for their medical help and service to the poor. As one biographer said, "Frederick's religion was essentially home-made."

At sixteen Frédéric had a crisis of faith. With the help of a priest at his school, he resolved his doubts and promised God to consecrate his life to the service of the Truth. He read widely in history, philosophy, and literature.

Frédéric studied law at the University of Paris in obedience to his father's wishes. At first deeply homesick, he found his way to a group of Catholic students; they formed a debating society. They shared many ideals of the Enlightenment: they believed in liberty and democracy, and they recognized that population growth and industrialization were radically changing French society. But many thinkers who shared these beliefs were antichurch and anti-Christian. It was at a debate with these thinkers that Frédéric and his friends were given a new challenge.

✦ ✦ ✦

You ask about Frédéric Ozanam. You have read about him, then? Frédéric and the founding of the Saint Vincent de Paul Society. It is long ago now. I was young then, in the first heady years of adult freedom. An exciting and dangerous time for a young man. Yet God guided us, and we came to understand the traps that lay around us. You do not understand?

Well, in the Romantic era, young people were taken with high ideals and lofty emotions. Some wanted to be great writers like Alexandre Dumas, or they were swept into rapture over the music of Beethoven or Chopin. Or they had tempestuous romances and fought duels. All wanted to accomplish great things.

Did Frédéric, too? Of course! But Frédéric, from among us all, had the sacred fire. He already knew his calling from God. And he had the self-discipline to make his dream a reality.

Let me tell you what happened a few nights before the Saint Vincent de Paul Society was formed. We were at our weekly debate, our so-called "Conferences on History." On this evening, Pierre Fontaine, an ardent follower of the philosophies of Saint-Simon and Voltaire, led the opposition.

"These times," he said, "are like the final days of Rome. The emperor and his court did not believe in their own gods. They pretended belief to appease the common people. Today's priests and bishops do not believe in God either. The clergy are greedy and self-serving hypocrites. The Catholic church ignores the needs of the poor."

Hurrahs and clapping rose from Fontaine's side of the hall. But Frédéric did not seem aware of the shouting. He was instead concentrating intently on Fontaine's words. As I think of him now, that is what I remember about him. He could focus with enormous intensity on a subject. Even though it was my turn to debate, Frédéric was incising Fontaine's arguments in his memory so that he might answer each step in order.

Fontaine mopped his brow in the heat of the overcrowded hall and pulled out a newspaper. "Have you read the editorial in last week's *Holy Faith?*"

I let out a groan. I had read the piece and knew what was coming. I was both nervous about the unruly crowd and angry with Fontaine already. I prided myself then on my debating skills. But when our opponents reviled the church and slandered her people, I would grow belligerent. That, of course, made me less effective at debate.

Frédéric leaned close to me. "Auguste, with your kind permission, I should like to speak tonight."

I nodded, half in frustration, half in relief.

Fontaine read, "'We have an answer for these philosophical upstarts who daily press us with the need for change. We can wholeheartedly say yes to change! Let us send these revolutionaries bent on destroying France to prison! That will be a change, if you like! Then the true, noble, and Catholic France can live in peace.'"

Fontaine bowed. "I give place to the true and noble Catholics. Who will be our debater tonight? Auguste le Taillandier, Paul Lemanche, or Frédéric Ozanam?"

Frédéric stood up to a chorus of hoots and catcalls. Oh! They called him the vilest of names! Yet he simply waited for the hall to calm down, studying people with that dark-eyed gaze of his. Here is an amazing thing about Frédéric. I never once heard him speak rudely to anyone. He did not care how other people saw him. Frédéric was attached to the Truth alone. And of that he was the sure-footed messenger.

Frédéric always knew the right moment, just before silence, to begin speaking. He bowed to the audience and said, "Allow me a brief introduction. We are all the children of the French Revolution and its aftermath, of the Napoleonic Years and the restored monarchy. Is this not so?"

"Yes!" answered several voices.

"And we agree that the times in which we live have a part in molding us. For us then, these national events are part of the intimate history of our families." Frédéric turned to Fontaine. "I agree with my esteemed opponent that—"

"Wha' does he mean, 'esteemed opponent'?" came a drunken voice from the top row of chairs. There was scattered laughter.

Frédéric said, "It means, my friend, that I can respect my opponent. I agree with part of his argument, and heartily disagree with the rest."

He turned to Fontaine. "These days do seem much like the end of the Roman Empire. Rome paid no heed to the needs of common people. The empire's leaders exhausted themselves in dissipation and vice. And France, like Rome, is weakened by worn-out institutions and the polluted living of our leaders and educated classes."

"Whose polluted living?" shouted a surly voice. Alphonse Renier, a member of

Fontaine's group, stood up. He had lived at Frédéric's first boarding house in Paris—an awful place. Renier used to sing obscene songs outside Frédéric's room every Sunday morning.

Frédéric said calmly, "If I may finish my point, you will see where it leads." Fontaine motioned Alphonse down.

"It is my contention that God ordained the fall of Rome to prepare his people for something new. The Christian church civilized Europe through the work of priests, monks, nuns, and teachers and through many anonymous people who led faithful lives. The Dark Ages were but the long pregnant pause before the birth of Christian Europe and the glories of the medieval world."

A chaos of catcalls and epithets erupted in the hall. The drunkard in the top row began to bawl out the "Marseillaise." What would come next? Rotten vegetables?

Fontaine stood, and the hall calmed down. He said, "You say the Church works for the common good and is allied to the people. Prove your point, monsieur."

Frédéric said, "Think of the monasteries, holding their precious codices, sheltering Plato and Aristotle along with Saint Augustine and the desert fathers, copying the mathematics and science of the ancient Greeks and Arabs. . . ."

Ah, Frédéric's propositions that night were tightly reasoned and impassioned. He spoke appealingly of Saint Dominic, Duns Scotus, and the great Saint Thomas Aquinas. Within minutes, Fontaine himself was listening. The rabble-rousers were absorbed in Frédéric's talk as though he were a respected professor, not a twenty-year-old student.

Frédéric said, "We were once a country with a meager population. Now the desperate multitudes leave their villages to find work in the cities. With each new morning, more of them arrive in Paris." He paused and his voice shook with emotion. "It is the battle of those who have nothing and those who have too much. It is the violent collision of opulence and poverty that makes the earth tremble under our feet."

Heads were nodding in agreement. Frédéric's voice rose. "But I say to you that the church must lead the way! Saint Francis Assisi, our own Saint Francis de Sales, and Saint Vincent de Paul knew this—"

"You know what I say, m'sieur?" It was the drunkard from the top row again. "I say th' Catholic church is full of horses' asses, and you're one too!"

Even Fontaine, worthy fellow in his way, looked pained. But Frédéric? A slow smile grew on his face.

"But, my friend, even an ass may serve God, as did Baalam's ass, when it saw the angel of God in the path and turned aside to save its unworthy master. And did not Our Lady ride an ass to Bethlehem as she carried within her body the light of the world? In such illustrious company, I am proud indeed—" and here he grinned and bowed, his arms spread wide, "—to be an ass."

Fontaine hooted a laugh. "Ozanam has got you there, La Roche, admit it!" he called up to the drunkard.

"Yes, yes," came the voice, punctuated by a hiccup. The entire hall laughed.

Fontaine said, "In past centuries, I admit, the church did marvelous things. Even I, an atheist, admit that Christ defended the poor. Saint Francis and Saint Vincent de Paul were great men, but they are dead. In the French church today I see only an ancient human institution whose single goal is self-preservation. I challenge you to give us an example of the church actively helping the poor in France now, this very day."

Frédéric paused. Instantly, Fontaine saw he had a foothold.

"Monsieur Ozanam," he said, "you talk a fine fight. But what are you yourself doing for the poor? If we witnessed genuine charity, even such as we—" Fontaine gestured to

the crowd around him, "might come to believe."

I saw Fontaine meet Frédéric's eyes. Some-
thing indescribable passed between them. Did
I see Frédéric's vulnerability or Fontaine's?
Was Fontaine admitting a secret longing for
God? I did not know, but now the crowd
caught on. The hoots and whistles started.

Frédéric was silent. How mortified I felt
for him! Why did he not speak? All of us
gave alms to the poor, though most of us
had little to spare. (I gave more, for my family was well-to-do.) Frédéric could have
talked about Sister Rosalie, for he visited the
slums with her. But it was common knowledge that Sister Rosalie worked without support from our aristocratic archbishop. At last
Frédéric, without a word, bowed. Fontaine
and his supporters gave a rousing cheer for
their side. They had won the final point.

Frédéric turned to us, and I saw distress in
his face. Francois Lallier, his best friend,
jumped to his feet and consoled him. Of
course, that only made it worse. The five of
us, Frédéric, Francois, Jules, Paul, and I,
waited for the hall to empty.

"Fontaine is right, my friends," said
Frédéric, and there were tears standing in his
eyes. "We defend our faith in debate, but we
have ignored the primary call of Christ to
serve the poor."

Paul Lemanche said eagerly, "Jules and I were speaking of this just last night."

Jules nodded. "We talked about a private meeting so that we might support each other's faith and help the poor."

Francois objected. "I agree we need to do more, but we all have our studies, and we are so few."

Frédéric put a hand on Francois's shoulder. "Let us pray about our course of action and talk at the next meeting." He turned to me. "Auguste, come with me. I have an idea."

Some details of that night's debate I might have lost over the years, but not what came next, for it was the single event that changed my life.

It was nearly midnight, a cold, clammy March night. We took the avenue out of the university district. We were loaded down, I with my coal and Frédéric with his firewood, all that he had for the season. We turned down a side street once, twice, and then into an alley. It was as if we had entered a different city. Rotting garbage was piled in corners. Wretched, crumbling buildings nearly toppled into each other above us.

"Sister Rosalie says the sun rarely shines here because the buildings lean so close," said Frédéric.

"No wonder it smells—Oh, help!" I lost my footing in the stream running down the center gutter. Frédéric caught my elbow. As I found my footing, I looked down. The slippery stream was raw sewage. "My—my God!" I stammered.

"Oui," said Frédéric bitterly. "Paris, the most civilized city on earth, is filled with poverty, greed, and misery."

He opened the door of an apartment building. The entrance stank of urine. We climbed the stairs. At the third floor we halted, gasping for breath. The stink in the closed hallway was revolting.

Frédéric knocked gently at a door. It opened a crack, and a woman looked out. Frédéric took off his hat and bowed formally, as if she were a fine lady. I did the same.

"Madame Louis, do you remember me? I visited last week with Sister Rosalie. My name is Frédéric Ozanam. This is Auguste le Taillandier. Please forgive us for calling at such a late hour."

"A moment," she said abruptly and closed the door. When she opened it again, I saw she was about forty, with dirty, disheveled hair and a blank face. She had wrapped herself in a shawl, but I was shocked to see bare legs and feet beneath her tattered skirt. I looked away, embarrassed. She was not fully dressed before strangers.

The moon was the only light in the room. A man sat on a single chair, bare from the waist up, his shivering body thin and wasted. Frédéric knelt before him.

"Monsieur Louis, how do you feel? Is the fever improved?"

"No," Monsieur Louis answered, then he coughed.

I looked around. The room was bare of furniture. A rope stretched from the single window frame to the opposite wall about five feet up. Hanging from the rope was a bag holding something. Was it bread? I could not be sure.

"We have brought firewood and coal," said Frédéric.

"What?" Madame Louis said blankly.

"For you and your family. To keep you warm," said Frédéric. He knelt and made the fire.

"Luc," she said immediately, "come to the fire." She coaxed him to stand, moved his chair nearer the fire, and settled him in it once more.

Now I could see. In one corner was a pile of straw and rags. Was that their bed? Then I jumped, for I saw movement. Rats? But, no, a bare leg appeared, then an arm. Children. Three of them. They held rags to their fronts as they stood up.

The smallest one, a boy of four, said "Marie, is it a dream?"

"Hush," said his sister. They approached the fire, drawn by its dancing light and warmth. I saw delight in their pinched faces. My heart contracted. Oh, pitiful ones!

"You came with Sister Rosalie?" asked Madame Louis.

"Yes," said Frédéric.

Madame Louis watched her husband and children gathered by the fire. It took her a moment to find the right words. "Thank you," she said at last.

"We will come again next week. God bless you and your family," said Frédéric.

"Yes." I found my voice for the first time, "God bless you." Madame Louis looked at me. A glimmer—was it of humor?—crossed her face. "The silent one," she said. I blushed and Frédéric grinned. We left and walked without words until we reached the main avenue.

Frédéric said, "The bag tied to the rope is to keep the food out of reach of rats."

Shocked, I stared at him.

"I saw you looking at it," he said.

My voice was shaking when I spoke. "I did not know it could be like this! It is inhuman! Their lives are torture!"

Almost absently Frédéric said, "You see how easy it is to be the Levite passing on the other side of the road. How could you know, Auguste? How many of us walk through the slums even in daylight?"

"Is their situation common?"

Frédéric met my eyes. "The slum districts in Paris go for miles, Auguste."

I was nearly crying. "The problem is so great! What can we do?"

Frédéric put a hand on my shoulder. "We will do what we can. We will go back each week and learn to know them. I think they need companionship and respect as much as they need food."

I swallowed hard. "But we offer so little! Perhaps Fontaine and the others are right. We need a new revolution."

"Fontaine and the others look for human solutions," said Frédéric. "We must think like Christ. We are to be a leaven to the whole society. Yes! We do little," his voice broke suddenly. "But God will honor what we do."

Then a terrible thought occurred to me. "Frédéric, I am from a comfortable family. Am I the rich man of the Gospels, overloaded with goods, unable to pass through the needle's eye?"

Frédéric smiled. "Your heart opened at the sight of their misery. The knowledge of them changes everything, does it not?"

In truth, I was so overcome I could only nod.

Frédéric watched me for a moment. "You are not like me, you know. I study the law to fulfill my father's wishes. You truly love the law. It is your vocation, Auguste. When you are a lawyer, work for the poor. Ask for their prayers instead of their coins. It will be worth more to you in the end, anyway."

We walked on in silence, though I was still trembling within. Back at my rooms, I climbed into bed, aware suddenly of the luxury of clean sheets and blankets, of my chair and desk, the heavy curtains that kept out the cold.

The next Tuesday we had the first meeting of the Saint Vincent de Paul Society. We did what all Vincentians have done since. We prayed together, and took up a collection that was divided equally among us. We went out in pairs; each pair befriended one particular family or person, returning to help them many times.

Ah now, I have talked about me, not about Frédéric. But I hope I have given you a sampling of his gracious character. And do you know, our Society in this year of 1881, is in twenty-eight different countries? Frédéric knew that all would be well for the Society if we trusted in God to lead the way, and that is what we have done. Frédéric would be pleased.

✦ ✦ ✦

Frédéric Ozanam finished his law studies and returned to Lyon after the death of his father. Two years later, his mother died. He continued to read widely and was soon offered a position teaching literature at the University of Paris, which was his dream. He married Amalie Soulacroix, a happy marriage that produced one daughter, Marie.

By the late 1840s, Frédéric's health began a long decline. He traveled around Europe and encouraged the founding of Saint Vincent de Paul Societies. He was pleased to hear of the founding of the Saint Vincent de Paul Society in Saint Louis, Missouri. He died of kidney disease at the age of forty. The Saint Vincent de Paul Society has spread worldwide.

The Arithmetic of Love

Archbishop Oscar Romero

*O*scar Romero was born in the mountain village of Caudal Barrio in El Salvador in 1917. His father, Santos, was the local postman and telegraph operator. Oscar went to school, then at twelve was apprenticed to a local carpenter, a job he enjoyed. When Oscar said he wanted to be a priest, he was sent to a minor seminary in San Miguel, a seven-hour trip by donkey. He studied theology in Rome and was ordained a priest in 1942. Back home, Oscar became secretary for the diocese of San Miguel, co-editor of its newspaper, and pastor for the cathedral, where he encouraged Catholic lay organizations. Romero became a well-known radio preacher; the people loved him.

Romero read carefully the documents of the Second Vatican Council and the Medellín Conference, the bishops' meeting that attempted to meld council ideas with the Latin American church. A traditionalist by nature, Oscar Romero did not agree with all the Vatican changes, but he was committed to the basic ideas, including increased lay participation.

By 1974, when he became bishop of Santiago de Maria, conditions in El Salvador were worsening. The population of El Salvador had quadrupled since the year of Romero's birth. Fourteen wealthy families controlled fifty percent of the land, leaving the landless *campesinos* without means of income except at harvest. Civil war broke out, with a revolutionary group trying to wrest power from the government and the families. The army believed that ninety percent of the people supported the rebels, so they began a reign of terror. Romero talked to government officials in private, but he believed that the church should not become involved politically. Soon, priests as well as laypeople were being murdered.

When Romero was named archbishop of El Salvador in 1977, most priests were disappointed, believing that Romero would simply continue the status quo. Within days of his installation, however, death squads murdered a priest friend and two others. Viewing their bodies, Oscar Romero's stance changed. Soon he became the most powerful voice in El Salvador to speak out against the government.

✦   ✦   ✦

It was after one in the afternoon when Oscar and Salvador reached the Barrazza home. Eugenia was out in the kitchen cooking. She called an *"Hola!"* when she heard them come in. Their eight-year-old daughter, Virginia, ran to Oscar and hugged him. He sat down in his favorite chair, took off his shoes, and allowed himself to let out a sigh.

"You sound tired, *mi amigo,*" said Salvador.

Oscar nodded. He looked up at Salvador. His friend was tall, with graying hair and glasses. Somehow, over the years, they had come to look alike. Strangers sometimes mistook them for brothers. They were *compadres*. He was Virginia's godfather; he was a co-parent with Salvador and Eugenia.

"What would you like to drink today? Campari?"

Oscar rubbed his ear. "No, scotch today."

Salvador disappeared. Oscar watched TV with Virginia. Her favorite show was on—he often arrived in time to see the puppet show on Sunday, after Mass at the basilica. The simply told stories were comforting to him. The moral choices were clear, and the "bad guy" was always defeated quickly.

Mass today had lasted longer than usual, from nine in the morning till one in the afternoon. He had preached a long time, reading off the toll of dead for this week, 108 people. Whole families had been murdered in the villages that the government suspected of supporting revolutionary forces.

Toward the end of his homily, he addressed the soldiers responsible for the killing. He knew some of them would listen to the radio broadcast. "Brothers, you are part of our own people. You kill your own *campesino* brothers and sisters. God's law must prevail: Thou shalt not kill! No soldier is obliged to obey an order against the law of God. No one has to fulfill an immoral law. It is time to obey your consciences rather than the orders of sin. The church cannot remain silent before such abomination. In the name of God and in the name of this suffering people, whose laments rise to heaven each day more tumultuous, I beg you, I beseech you, I order you in the name of God: *stop the repression!*"

He received death threats on a regular basis, of course, in phone calls or anonymous notes. But last week the papal nuncio of Costa Rica called. The nuncio's staff was hearing rumors of a plot to kill him. The foreign minister of Nicaragua called the same day to offer him refuge.

"I must remain with my people and face the risks of the moment," Oscar had told him. He had to stand with the people. He pictured the woman who had come to his office yesterday, begging for help to locate her son, who had disappeared. A new fear—fear for his own life—swelled in him. Now death might come as a knock on his door. Death might come as a stranger in the crowds, a face with eyes hardened against pleas for mercy. *One minus one is zero,* he thought. *I am only one man.*

That same day he had begun his final arrangements. He signed papers so that there would be a quorum of priests in San Salvador to name a priest to serve in his place, someone to help the people until a new archbishop could be named. He also wrote a long letter to Raul, his foster son. Oscar had raised Raul and seen him married. He had baptized Raul's children.

Salvador came with the scotch.

"Thank you," said Oscar, taking a sip of the drink.

Salvador hesitated, standing before him. "Are you not feeling well?"

Oscar rubbed his ear again. "An earache. It's nothing much."

"I'll drive you to the doctor on Monday," said Salvador.

"I can drive myself," said Oscar. He knew Salvador had a busy week ahead at his shoe factory.

A smile lit Salvador's face. "Mi amigo, we both know that the Holy Spirit did not give you the gift of good driving. Let me do it."

Salvador was teasing. Oscar laughed a little and nodded. He watched Virginia. She saw him looking her way, came around the back of his chair, and hugged him from behind. It was a sweet comfort.

"We are ready," called Eugenia, as she brought in the roast chicken.

Oscar looked from face to face around the table. What good people they were! He loved them all, but love for them brought also a burgeoning pain within. He did not talk, but ate his food in silence.

He had been on a retreat for priests two weeks ago. There was time for prayer and confession, and also for frank talk. The comments of his brother priests were much the same as they had always been.

"You are sometimes irritable, Monseñor," said Father Filippe. "You embarrass us with your short, angry answers."

Father Juan, an older man, had seen much terror in his three villages. His voice was quiet when he spoke. "You do not share your burdens with us, Monseñor. You hold everything to yourself. It is too much for one man to carry."

"I agree," said Father Angelo. "Sometimes you seem overwhelmed with the problems we face. Perhaps you should scale back your activities."

Oscar sighed. Sometimes he wondered if he had made any progress at all in the spiritual life. He was still poor at delegating responsibility, a perfectionist and overly scrupulous, too.

"Oscar," said Salvador, "Did you hear what Eugenia said?"

Oscar looked over at Eugenia. "I'm sorry. What did you ask?"

"I asked why an announcement in the newspaper said that you will be celebrating Mass tomorrow at six o'clock in the hospital chapel."

Oscar shrugged. "I'm not sure. The announcement didn't come from my office."

Eugenia looked at him with worry in her face. Oscar took off his glasses and rubbed his eyes. What could he say to them? *I don't know how much longer I will be with you.* Could he admit to them—and in front of little Virginia, too—that he was terrified of the savage death so many had suffered? He thought back to his installation as archbishop of El Salvador. Fr. Rutillo Grande had planned the great celebration. It was less than a week after his installation when he stood over Father Rutillo's body, beside the bodies of the old man and the boy who had been with him. All three had been shot in the head. But the death squad had driven a truck over Father

Rutillo's face to make their message clear. Oscar straightened in his chair. No, he must not allow himself to think this way.

He said, "Did I ever tell you about my friend in seminary in Rome? His name was Rafael Valladares." He talked about Rafael and several good friends he had and how they helped him. It was calming to speak of them. "And you, too, all you Barrazzas, you have been so good to me."

Eugenia smiled at him, pleased. "You helped us when I was sick, and we helped you when you were sick. God has blessed you with many friendships."

Salvador touched Oscar's arm. "It helps in these dark days, eh?"

Sudden tears sprang to Oscar's eyes. He rubbed them.

Eugenia said quietly, "It is as Scripture says, 'We see in a glass darkly,' That is El Salvador today, with secrets and murder and the smoke of burning villages."

Oscar glanced at Virginia. She was looking from one of them to the next with fear in her eyes. He said, "Enough of grown-up problems. How are you doing in arithmetic, Virginia?"

She took a deep breath. "Monseñor, I still do not like it! The teacher keeps saying, 'You can trust numbers. Memorize the answers and they will always be the same.'" She glared around the table. "Well, I think that is boring!"

Oscar laughed. "Be patient. Some day you may find the rigor of numbers helpful, even comforting. Arithmetic can always be put to good use. I used it all the time when I was a carpenter's apprentice to build my chairs and tables."

"And coffins, too," said Virginia. "You made coffins." For a moment, no one said anything. Virginia looked around the table. "What is wrong?"

"Nothing, my dear," said Oscar. "You are right. I did use arithmetic to build coffins."

It was late. Oscar had his bedside lamp on. His room was behind the rear wall of the hospital chapel, near to the Blessed Sacrament. The room was secluded and simple. The only thing was, its thin walls would not keep out bullets. When he heard sounds outside these days, sleep was long in coming. He prayed the Night Prayers in his breviary.

"Protect us, Lord, as we stay awake; watch over us as we sleep, that awake we may keep watch with Christ, and asleep, rest in his peace."

An odd sensation filled him when he read the words of Simeon in the Temple when he saw the baby Jesus. "Lord, now your servant can go in peace; your word has been fulfilled. My own eyes have seen the salvation you have prepared in the sight of every people: a light to reveal you to the nations and the glory of your people Israel."

He turned out the light and lay in the dark and the silence, waiting for the presence of God. When he was a boy, God did not often come to him with anthems or with words in his mind. God was simply with him. God's silent presence was itself his comfort and his shelter.

But tonight he felt alone, suspended before the threatening future. He thought of the bodies left by the roadside with signs pinned to them. *Don't touch this traitor or you'll be next.* He swallowed the hard tightness in his throat. Sweat broke out on his face and arms. He gripped the sheet of his bed and begged God for grace to withstand this moment of panic.

It came to him that this was how the prophet Jeremiah must have felt at the bottom of his well, having been thrown there for speaking the truth. And Elijah, too, hiding in his cave for fear that King Ahab and Queen Jezebel would kill him. Of course, Jesus himself was alone, even before the night when the disciples ran away. James and John wanted to sit at his right and left hand in the Kingdom. "You do not know what you are asking," Jesus told them. "Are you willing to drink the cup I have to drink?"

"Mercy, Lord," he prayed and waited, breathing hard. Slowly, slowly, mercy came to him. Timely mercy, bodily mercy. His rolling fear began to ease. He saw that he did not have to do anything now; he need only accept this waiting. He felt calm and sleepy, like a tired child. Tomorrow he would have Salvador drive him out to Santa Tecla for confession. That was the last thing he needed to do. He slid into sleep without noticing.

Oscar rose early for prayers and then went for a few hours of study with his fellow priests. That could not help but revive him. The priests were mostly young men, and they had a youthful energy, a life force that helped him. It was a pleasure to study the Scriptures with them. Monday was normally his morning off, but that did not matter. At 3:30, Salvador picked him up for the doctor's appointment. He told Salvador about wanting confession. Did Salvador think they could drive to Santa Tecla after the doctor's appointment and get back to the hospital by 5:30 to prepare for Mass?

"Yes, if we are careful," said Salvador. He looked at Oscar. "Didn't you go to confession two weeks ago?"

"Yes—but I want to stand before God with my soul cleansed."

Salvador looked at him for a long moment, then nodded.

Oscar felt reassured at the sight of his confessor. Father Azcue had seen much in his long life. He had a deep compassion for people no matter what their situation. His confession did not take long.

"God asks me to trust him, and sometimes I cannot. I ask God's grace to help me stand firm even when I feel afraid."

Father Azcue put his hand on Oscar's shoulder. "I know you believe that death is imminent, Oscar, and it may be. Your disposition must be to give your life for God, whatever comes." He stopped a moment, his voice shaking. "You will be given God's grace no matter what happens. God will be with you because you have lived for him."

Afterward, Oscar felt relieved, almost happy. He embraced Father Azcue and said quietly, "Pray for me, Father." The old man nodded wordlessly. Then Oscar and Salvador were on the road back to the city.

He took time putting on his vestments. Purple for Lent. Even the statues in the chapel were veiled in purple. Catholics often saw Lent as a time for penance and fasting, a hard season. "But Lent means spring," Oscar said to himself as he put on the chasuble. "I must remind them of that."

Tonight was a memorial Mass for Sarita Pinto, who had died the year before. Her son, Jorge Pinto, ran *El Independiente,* a newspaper that was bombed two weeks ago. He began the Mass. Jorge's wife and children were there along with family and friends, as were the sisters from the hospital. But not Jorge. Oscar smiled a little to himself. Jorge was running late again.

As he read Psalm 23 antiphonally with the people, a calm settled over him. "Though I walk through the dark valley, I fear nothing, for you are at my side."

He thought and felt his way through each word of the Gospel of John. "The hour has come for the Son of Man to be glorified. Very truly, I tell you, unless a grain of wheat falls into the earth and dies, it remains just a single grain; but if it dies, it bears much fruit. . . . Now my soul is troubled. And what should I say—'Father, save me from this hour'? No, it is for this reason that I have come to this hour."

He raised the book above his head. "This is the Gospel of the Lord."

"Praise to you, Lord Jesus Christ," said the people.

In his homily, Oscar spoke of Sarita Pinto's life, dedicated to building the Kingdom of God. He said, "You just heard in Christ's Gospel that one must not love oneself so much as to avoid getting involved in the risks of life that history demands of us. Those who try to fend off danger will lose their lives. But those who, out of love for Christ, give themselves to the service of others will live, like the grain of wheat that dies, but only apparently. If the seed did not die, it would remain alone. Only in undoing itself does it produce the harvest."

He looked out at the people. He knew them, he knew their lives, and they knew him. Indeed, they shared life together, and that life, he thought, could never be reduced to zero. He received the bread and wine. He placed them on the altar and faced the people. A hot wind blew in the open doors of the chapel. Oscar looked. A man stood outside, waiting for someone, perhaps.

Oscar raised his hands. "Pray, my brothers and sisters, that our sacrifice may be acceptable to God, the almighty Father." At the edge of his vision, he saw the man move.

✦ ✦ ✦

The gunman at the door fired a single shot, which hit Oscar Romero in the chest. He was carried to the nearest hospital, but he died a few moments later.

Jorge Pinto, arriving late, was able to give the police a description of the shooter and of the police who watched the murderer escape and did nothing. But the case was never resolved. The unrest and killings continued into 1992, when the civil war finally ended. When people poured into San Salvador to celebrate, they carried pictures of Oscar Romero and stopped to pray at his grave in the cathedral. Although the church is still considering whether to beatify Oscar Romero, he is already a saint in the hearts of the people of El Salvador.